THE BUILDING BLOCKS OF SALES ENABLEMENT

Mike Kunkle

Alexandria, VA

24 23 22 21 1 2 3 4 5

ATD Press is an internationally renowned source of insightful and practical information on talent development, training, and professional development.

ATD Press
1640 King Street
Alexandria, VA 22314 USA

Ordering information: Books published by ATD Press can be purchased by visiting ATD's website at td.org/books or by calling 800.628.2783 or 703.683.8100.

Library of Congress Control Number: 2021939799

ISBN-10: 1-952157-62-5
ISBN-13: 978-1-952157-62-2
e-ISBN: 978-1-952157-63-9

ATD Press Editorial Staff
Director: Sarah Halgas
Manager: Melissa Jones
Content Manager, Sales Enablement: Kimberly McAvoy
Developmental Editor: Kathryn Stafford
Text Design: Shirley E.M. Raybuck, ATD, and Kathleen Dyson
Cover Design: Rose Richey

Printed by BR Printers, San Jose, CA

Contents

Foreword to Sales Leaders

By David Brock

About a year ago, Mike Kunkle told me that he was writing a book called *The Building Blocks of Sales Enablement* and asked me if I would write a foreword geared toward sales leaders. Glibly, I accepted. Fast forward to the present—I have a draft of the book in my email and a request from Mike to make good on my commitment.

Frankly, I'm amazed by how much he was able to cover in a relatively small number of pages. I suspect that if I'd attempted a similar effort, the *Encyclopedia Britannica* would have looked like the condensed version of my book.

However, as I reflected on what I'd read, I realized that this foreword couldn't be geared toward a single audience. Front-line sales managers should read it with certain objectives and perspectives in mind, while sales executives, CROs, and top sales leaders will read it with a slightly different perspective. And then there are the other leaders in the sales organization, particularly those tasked with leading the sales enablement organization. (Thankfully, my friend, Tamara Schenk, is taking care of that.)

So, this foreword addresses two types of sales leaders: the front-line manager and sales executives.

Front-Line Sales Managers

Sales enablement is, possibly, your most important partner in maximizing the performance of each person on the team. Sales enablement provides the resources critical to your ability to execute with customers. Your role is to help each person on the team leverage these resources for maximum impact. You do this through coaching and development and by leveraging other resources in the company.

One of the more important things Mike does to help sales managers is to outline how each part fits together to create high-impact sales. We need to look at everything that influences sales performance from a systems point of view—how they interrelate and how we use the "system" to help address performance and drive success. Mike's framework for looking at the complete set of tools, processes, and programs enables us to leverage those that produce the greatest impact on performance.

As a front-line sales manager, you also have a framework you can take back to the sales enablement team, as you need new things to help you and your people achieve your goals. Sales enablement also provides programs and tools to help you develop as a leader. Cultivate a tight relationship with your sales enablement team and leverage them to help you and your team hit your numbers!

Sales Executives

You are responsible for maximizing the performance of your organization by executing the company strategy in the face of the customer. The framework Mike provides in this book will help ensure you have all the bases covered for your organization.

Maximizing sales performance is about doing the "whole job." Too many leaders and organizations fail because they don't recognize this fact. Instead, they continue to blindly do what they've done in the past. Mike's framework allows you to understand the interrelationships between each part of the selling system. It highlights the leverage points—those things that have the greatest impact on performance—and helps you identify things you should be doing but may have missed. This framework provides a holistic view of how the organization most effectively and efficiently achieves its goals and drives revenue.

When things are working, we often don't pay much attention to their details. We just stick to the status quo. But the challenge is, what do we do when things aren't working as well as they should? What do we do when the markets are disrupted?

Where do we start when looking at how we adjust, respond, and drive performance? This book provides the tools we need to start identifying and addressing these issues. It helps us figure out where to start, what we might be missing, what might have the most impact.

For sales leaders at any level, *The Building Blocks of Sales Enablement* lives up to its title. It provides a complete view of the systems, processes, tools, programs, and training critical for maximizing sales performance. It helps you understand how they interrelate and where you could focus to address performance issues. It's a book you should keep at close reach and refer to as you grow the capabilities of your organization and each person on your team.

Foreword to Sales Enablement Leaders

By Tamara Schenk

The world of enablement is small, but true expertise, passion, focus, and visions about a topic last forever. Mike and I met first online and then in person at a Forrester sales enablement conference in Phoenix back in 2012. At that conference, we bonded over our passion for sales enablement with our mutual friend Dave Brock, who wrote the other foreword for this book.

We connected immediately through Mike's holistic approach to sales enablement and his way of thinking in systems and providing ambitious frameworks. (I wouldn't have been surprised if this book had been called *Frameworks Matter*.)

We often joked that I got the diamonds and Mike got the building blocks (my sales enablement book leverages a diamond framework), but as I said the other day, these building blocks are actually worth diamonds. Regardless of the framework that enablement practitioners and leaders choose, what's most important is that they work with a comprehensive framework in the first place.

Frameworks matter. Frameworks provide a frame of reference for your work as an enablement leader. They model reality in an aggregated and simplified way without losing essential dimensions, and that's what makes all the difference. There are no shortcuts to enablement success. It needs to be set up in a strategic, formal, and holistic way that addresses all relevant dimensions, including sales readiness and sales engagement, buyers and their journeys, sales managers, sales processes, and methodologies.

A "three steps to success" model (no, that's not a framework) that shows an overly simplified reality without representing all the relevant dimensions is not helpful. It will simply land you in irrelevance—you might implement some activities, but they probably won't move the sales performance needle.

Why is this the case? Comprehensive and complete frameworks are mission critical because they allow you to apply their principles and concepts to your specific context and adjust them accordingly.

During my time as research director at CSO Insights, I learned a lot from five global enablement studies that we conducted. We found that if you implement enablement activities without meeting your senior executives' expectations or connecting your enablement strategy to the sales strategy, you won't be able to show how those efforts positively affected the business. We also found that more than 50 percent of enablement teams were investing in enablement *without* showing positive results.

In a good economy this isn't as noticeable. However, fast-forward to a global pandemic and it's not a good situation to be in. As the pandemic hit the economy hard, the truth came to the surface, and many enablement practitioners lost their jobs. It was the kind of situation when the CFO became the "CFNo."

Now, as the economy begins to recover, it's evident that enablement is more important than ever. In fact, if we set it up right, strategically and holistically, this could become the decade of enablement! Enablement could drive sales and customer success in this new buyer-driven, remote-first world.

The challenges in sales did not change just because we started working remotely most of the time. In fact, this only amplified the existing challenges surrounding our lack of foundational selling skills. If salespeople lack all the elements of personal meetings, they'll have a much harder time engaging their prospects and customers remotely.

Now, making this the decade of enablement requires a well-thought-out approach. Luckily, *The Building Blocks of Sales Enablement* contains a comprehensive framework that covers everything you need to think about!

Implementing this framework in your context requires critical thinking, creative thinking, and system thinking. In a world that's more and more driven by AI, it's more important than ever to be able to think critically, question assumptions, and imagine in more than three dimensions. It's fantastic that intelligent tools can enhance your effectiveness. However, to be truly successful leaders, we need to remain the masters and our tools the servants. Once this capability is in place and encouraged, it will provide the proper foundation for creative thinking and system thinking to make all the difference in our fast-pacing, complex world.

I encourage you to read this book and implement these building blocks in your organization for five important reasons:

1. **A holistic and strategic approach to sales enablement and its maturity levels** is the foundation of this excellent book and the prerequisite for your success. Enablement is cross-functional, so you'll need to effectively navigate across multiple functions (including marketing, product, L&D, various operations teams, customer success, and IT). You also need a shared vision of future success, which you inspire and uphold and implement in different phases and maturity levels. Mike's building blocks show you how to do that.
2. **It has a buyer-oriented perspective.** Those of you who know my work know that I am always focused on a customer-oriented approach, ensuring that enablement equips customer-facing professionals so they can be effective along every stage of the buyers' journey. Mike's building blocks begin there, with the buyers' acumen and buyer engagement content.
3. **Content is a lot more than marketing content.** Speaking of content, another aspect I love about Mike's work is that he believes there is no such thing as just "marketing content." Instead, he also discusses buyer engagement content (both are customer-facing), as well as sales readiness content and sales support content (which are internal content categories). I pointed that out in my book, and Mike has enhanced this distinction here. It's mission critical to understand and address each content category differently because they serve different purposes.
4. **Sales coaching and sales manager enablement are an integral part of the framework.** This is another area where Mike and I always inspire each other. The best enablement efforts always include sales coaching to drive adoption and reinforcement. In doing so, enablement leaders have to collaborate with sales leadership and sales managers from the very beginning, ideally providing specific tracks in sales manager onboarding and readiness services. If sales managers don't coach at all or are not in line with the enablement initiative, you put the whole

initiative at risk. So, even if you have to add yet another function to your orchestration efforts, it's absolutely worth doing so.

5. **It's grounded in processes and methodologies.** And, last but not least, Mike's framework formally implements sales processes and methodologies. Of course, the sales process is aligned to the customer journey, and the sales methodologies are appropriate, given the selling scenarios.

This may all sound simple or self-evident; however, from many years as an analyst and consultant, I can tell you that it is not. Formally or even adaptively implementing sales processes using the appropriate methodologies is a rare thing. However, you need this foundation because your enablement efforts cannot exist in a vacuum. So, a robust and perfectly designed buyer-seller journey framework is mandatory for any enablement and sales success. Mike's building blocks provide an excellent approach to get it right.

Introduction

How We Got Here, With This Thing Called "Sales Enablement"

In 2019, the sales enablement profession saw more than 10,000 people with "sales enablement" in their title. (We know this because of Paul Krajewski's ongoing title searches on LinkedIn—his chart shows a hockey stick of explosive growth over the past few years.) So, sales enablement has finally become "a thing" (or at least it has in some vertical markets). It reminds me of the phenomenon where people work for years at their craft, but when their popularity hits a tipping point, they become an "overnight success."

But what is sales enablement? In essence, it's a function (or department), a title, and a growing body of knowledge about how to support sales forces effectively. Interestingly, without using the term *sales enablement,* I've been doing this work for years, and I know quite a few other early practitioners who cite the same path. As far as back as 1991, I was:

- Collaborating with marketing on messaging, collateral, campaigns, and promotions
- Working with HR and compensation leaders to ensure compensation programs and incentives fostered the sales behaviors and outcomes we wanted
- Designing and delivering training (often coordinating with corporate training leaders), including building sales onboarding programs that shortened ramp-up times and improved new-hire production
- Teaching both sales process and methodology
- Building job aids and sales tools
- Using the technology that existed at the time

- Conducting training and initiative evaluations to determine the effectiveness of our efforts and return on investment
- Training and engaging front-line sales managers to reinforce training and coach reps to mastery in support of this work

Sound familiar? It should. Although sales enablement frequently includes these activities, the profession still does not have a universal definition.

Multiple analysts not only cover sales enablement in their research, reports, and advisory services, they also define it—and each analyst has their own definition. Since I started writing this book and sourcing definitions, Forrester acquired SiriusDecisions, Korn Ferry acquired CSO Insights, and Gartner acquired TOPO, so there are fewer definitions today, but they still vary quite a bit. Here are several of today's definitions of sales enablement:

- **Gartner:** Sales enablement is the process of enabling sales teams to close more deals by providing them with the resources they need to be more effective. Resources may include tools, technology, training, content, or actionable strategies to sell your product or service to customers. High-performing sales enablement functions provide specific resourcing and supporting tools to simplify the selling process and reduce the burden on the salesperson. This leads to increased conversion rates.
- **Forrester:** The goal of sales enablement is to ensure sellers possess the skills, knowledge, assets, and process expertise to maximize every buyer interaction.
- **Sales Enablement Society:** Sales enablement ensures buyers are engaged at the right time and place with the right assets by well-trained, client-facing staff to provide a world-class experience along the customer's journey. While utilizing the right sales and performance management technologies in addition to synergizing cross-organizational collaboration, sales enablement optimizes the selling motion in order to increase pipeline, move opportunities forward, and win bigger deals more efficiently to drive profitable growth.
- **Association for Talent Development:** The goal of sales enablement is to increase the productivity of market-facing teams by providing ongoing and strategic resources throughout the buyer journey to drive business impact. It encompasses sales training, coaching, content creation, process improvement, talent development, and compensation, among other areas.

It's enough to make you dizzy, isn't it?

When you talk to practitioners, there is just as much variation. However, at a high level many seem to agree that the current state of sales enablement includes:

- Sales messaging
- Sales content to:
  - Attract, interest, and engage buyers
  - Answer buyer questions throughout their buying process
- Sales training and supporting materials and elements
- Sales technology and tools

So, let's look deeper. What is sales content? We have at least four types of content:

- **Marketing content:** This is what your marketing team designs to attract your targeted buyer personas to your company and website (through inbound marketing).
- **Buyer engagement content:** There are two types of buyer engagement content:
  - The first type is similar to marketing content, designed by marketing for use by sales reps when doing outbound prospecting to capture buyer interest and elicit a response.
  - The other type is collateral designed to meet the buying process exit criteria for your typical buyer personas. This collateral engages buyers by answering questions throughout the process and clarifying what buyers need to understand about your company, products, and services to make effective decisions.
- **Training content:** This is the content used to train your sales force, including new reps, incumbent reps, and front-line sales managers. Training content includes everything your reps and managers need to know and do to succeed, including product knowledge, buyer acumen, business acumen, sales process, and sales methodology.
- **Sales support content:** Included here are the playbooks, materials, job aids, cheat sheets, and tools that support your sales force in selling as your leadership team intends (using your sales process and sales methodology).

This describes sales enablement for most people in our profession, which means that this is also the starting point for thinking about how to evolve our sales enablement functions to truly support our sales organizations.

In addition to the varying analyst definitions and practitioner viewpoints, different organizations implement sales enablement differently. Many have begun to note that there are maturity models of sales enablement. Similar to the analysts' definitions, there are multiple models, but Table I-1 shows how I see them.

Table I-1. Sales Enablement Maturity Models

Maturity	Description
None	• "Leave them alone and let them sell" (Borrowed from David Bauders of SPARXiQ) • No effort; no impact on sales performance
Random	• Highly reactive, arbitrary acts of sales enablement • Fire fighting • Distracted by "bright shiny objects" • Unlikely to impact sales performance, other than luck
Informal	• Some structure, but not strategic, systemic, or scalable • Still somewhat reactive • Partly data-driven • Likely a limited impact on sales performance
Formal	• Sales enablement building blocks with a charter • Cross-functional collaboration • Supported by systems thinking • Strategic, structured, systemic, scalable, and measurable • Data-driven • Significant impact on sales performance
Adaptive	• A formal maturity level and performance consulting practices • A data-driven, diagnostic-based continuous focus on improving sales performance

How to Get the Most Out of This Book

I hope the need for this book is now clear. As a profession, we're not aligned on the way we define sales enablement, we're operating at a variety of maturity levels (some of which do not produce business results), and the fundamentals that many do align on are too basic to drive organizational performance improvement. To add to the confusion, even at the most simplified level, we use the term "content" to mean more than one thing.

I wrote *The Building Blocks of Sales Enablement* to help senior sales and sales enablement leaders effectively start or evolve a sales enablement function that delivers business results. But the process wasn't easy, for several reasons.

I didn't start in the field recently. I've been doing sales enablement since 1991, which means I have a lot of different experiences in varied organizations and have developed multiple frameworks, models, and systems that have helped me get great results. Capturing and codifying almost 30 years of work in a way that someone else can absorb and use has been a challenge unto itself—a fun one, but a challenge nonetheless.

The sales function is an ecosystem that exists within a larger organizational environment that has performance levers at the organization, function, position, and task levels. This means there are opportunities to align and improve performance at the company, department, and role levels. Because of this, I developed a systems approach to support the performance levers for sales enablement and improving sales performance. The interesting dilemma with systems work is that it's a culmination of separate parts that unify into a larger whole (where, when done well, the whole is greater than the sum of its parts). My building blocks of sales enablement are supported by four sales systems, and, due to the nature of the building blocks and the systems, there is some overlap.

The challenge lies in explaining the interplay between the blocks and the systems. For example, do I detail how sales enablement technology supports selling in the chapter on the sales technology building block? Or should I do it when sharing the Sales Training System, where I typically show how sales technology can support the 5 Stages of Sales Mastery and Behavior Change? Do I detail buyer engagement content in the Sales Readiness System, or in the corresponding building blocks chapter?

Here's what I finally settled on: I share the details and most in-depth content, whenever possible, in the building block chapters. And I've aligned the four systems (sales hiring, sales readiness, sales training, and sales management) as closely as I could to the building blocks.

The framework, collaboration, and communication practices are all intertwined with the systems:

- The building blocks represent a framework. They are the elements that must be in place for a sales force to function at its highest-possible level.
- Cross-functional collaboration and communication practices support the building blocks.
- The systems also support the building blocks, and you implement the building blocks through the systems you create.

When discussing the systems, I:

- Refer you to the building block chapters for more details whenever possible.
- Detail the content in the systems sections if there isn't a direct correlation to a building block chapter.

I'm not sure whether this will make sense until you get there, but when I refer to other chapters for the details, multiple times, at least you'll know my reasoning. It made more sense than asking you to dig into the details in more than one place. Since there is even some overlap between building blocks (buying process and sales process, for example), I occasionally make references between those chapters as well.

Lastly, you'll notice that some chapters are far shorter than others, and some are far more detailed. There is a logical reason for this. While each building block is important, some are more complex than others and require more explanation. For example, while the act of designing great sales playbooks, developing useful job aids, or customizing workflow performance support software is detailed work and critical for the success of the sales support content building block, explaining the concepts is rather simple—this book is not intended to be a complete guide for each of those things. By contrast, specifying the steps of the Sales Training System—with the embedded five stages of sales mastery and behavior change and the principles behind each element—requires more detail.

Also, since the act of enabling a sales force spans multiple functions, highly effective sales enablement leaders frequently collaborate with other departments and functional leaders. I've tried to detail a bit more about the building blocks that are typically owned by sales enablement, versus those where the detailed tasks are performed elsewhere.

If You Are a Sales Leader

First, see the foreword from Dave Brock for some great insight on the book from a sales leader perspective. In addition, here are some ways you might use this book to your advantage.

Start with a problem you're trying to solve. (It should be relatively easy to review the table of contents to find a related chapter).

- Are you implementing a new sales methodology and struggling to get adoption?
- Are buyers not responding well to the content that your reps are sharing?
- Are your reps pitching products rather than using a buyer-centric, problem-based prospecting approach?

Are you looking to establish or evolve a sales enablement function at your company? For example, at SPARXiQ, we have various assessments that can help you diagnose gaps in your sales force effectiveness. Then, using the results of the assessments, you can start implementing or refining the appropriate building blocks that best help you close the gaps identified. Similarly, if you'd prefer to do the work on your own, you can use the building blocks or the four systems in this book as a diagnostic, assessing your organization against the best practices to create an action plan.

Keep in mind that this book provides a detailed look at the moving pieces and parts of a sales enablement function that's operating at a formal maturity level. Be prepared for some detail. Real and significant organizational performance improvement doesn't result from the "harder, faster, longer, louder" method of sales leadership. It takes a disciplined execution of smart performance improvement initiatives, which is sorely lacking in many organizations.

As you work to develop and implement solutions—hopefully in partnership with a sales enablement leader—stay focused and allow your sales enablement leader to execute on your agreed-upon plans. Far too often, sales enablement does not produce the desired results because someone (usually a senior executive or senior sales leader) is easily distracted by "bright shiny objects" or flavor-of-the-month thinking, or they'll overreact to the last thing that went wrong. This behavior derails the good plans that are in place in favor of new, knee-jerk initiatives that address a one-off problem. It's OK to adjust and pivot strategies when things change or new information becomes available. But if this happens too frequently, your sales enablement efforts will not produce results for you.

Remember that most impactful sales enablement projects are change management initiatives in disguise. As the senior sales leader, you set the tone and influence the sales culture. If you don't foster a culture of accountability, coaching, and ongoing development, you may be part of the problem instead of the solution. In ATD's *2019 State of Sales Training* research report, 59 percent of survey respondents cited "Salespeople are not held accountable for applying skills learned in training" as the top barrier to training effectiveness.

If You Are a Sales Enablement Leader

First, see the foreword from Tamara Schenk for some great insight on the book from a sales enablement perspective. In addition, here are some ways that you might use this book to your advantage.

Use the building blocks as a diagnostic tool and a road map. Assess your function against the full building blocks framework to determine what you are currently doing very well, and where you can improve.

Use logic to prioritize initiatives based on the potential impact:

- If you don't have a charter in place, start there. Getting alignment about how you define sales enablement, which functions you will collaborate with, what you'll focus on, and how you will measure success will serve you very well.
- Are you implementing a sales methodology? First, ensure it's the right one for your business. No matter how well you implement the methodology, if it's the wrong one it's unlikely to make an impact.
- Are you launching a new product? Taking a scenario-based approach to product training, creating a certification, and ensuring buyer-centric, problem- versus product-focused messaging, will be more effective than revamping your sales management operating rhythm at that time.
- Prioritizing is key. Let's say you have a sales force of 100 with 5 percent turnover and only plan to hire replacements. In that case, revamping your new-hire sales onboarding program will not have as much impact as shifting the current sales team to a buyer-centric, value selling methodology that includes quarterly business reviews and top-notch strategic account management practices.

No one can implement all of the building blocks or systems at once. It's like the old joke about how you eat an elephant—one bite at a time. Using a diagnostic approach and the logic outlined here, work to get the building blocks and systems in place—one (or two) at a time—based on your resources, time, and budget and always with an eye toward impact and supporting strategic objectives.

Lastly, while this project and all the related frameworks, models, methods, practices, and systems may feel weirdly like part of my family after all these years, it helps to keep a sense of perspective. This is a peek into how my mind works, and the work I've done over the years that has truly produced great results for me. But I always remember something that I read in one of Tony Robbins's books years ago (although I'm not sure I fully understood it at the time). I later came to learn that the quote originated from mathematician Alfred Korzybski in the 1930s: "The map is not the territory."

The Farnam Street blog (fs.blog), which is an absolutely wonderful resource for critical thinking and decision making, offers a far more eloquent description than I can. In short, the building blocks framework is not reality—it is a representation of reality. It shows you where the streets and buildings are, but not the potholes and raised sidewalk blocks or missing grates. The work you do in bringing it to life inside your company and with your sales force is the reality and where the magic happens. I hope my map helps you get where you want to go. But the real work—the work that matters and produces results—well, that's all you.

1 The Building Blocks of Sales Enablement

A Formal Approach With Systems Thinking

To help senior sales leaders and sales enablement leaders effectively start or evolve a sales enablement function that delivers business results, I focus on a formal maturity model, with the sales enablement building blocks, supported by systems thinking (Figure 1-1).

Here is a description of each block in the building blocks framework:

- **Buyer acumen:** In this building block you identify your buyer personas and their COIN-OP (challenges, opportunities, impacts, needs, objectives, and priorities), the problems they are trying to solve, what outcomes are they trying to achieve, and what metrics matter to each. This also covers their typical buying process, including objectives, tasks, and exit criteria per process stage.
- **Buyer engagement content:** There are two types of buyer engagement content:
  - The first is similar to the marketing content sales reps use when doing outbound prospecting to capture buyer interest and elicit a response.
  - The other type is designed to meet the exit criteria for your typical buyer personas as they progress through their buying process. This

collateral engages buyers by answering their questions and clarifying questions about your company, products, and services so they can make effective buying decisions.

- **Sales support content:** This includes the playbooks, materials, job aids, cheat sheets, and tools that support your sales force in selling as your leadership team intends (using your sales process and sales methodology).
- **Sales hiring:** In this building block, you collaborate to create a plan and process to source, recruit, hire, and promote sales reps and managers who succeed in their chosen role.
- **Sales training:** Here, you build a training and development plan to support your sales force. This includes sales onboarding and ongoing training that supports business objectives, teaching sales process and sales methodology, developing ongoing training to close sales competency gaps, and training and enabling sales managers. For best results, you will use a Sales Training System to train, sustain knowledge, practice and develop skills, transfer those skills, and coach to mastery.

Figure 1-1. Sales Enablement Building Blocks With Sales Support Services

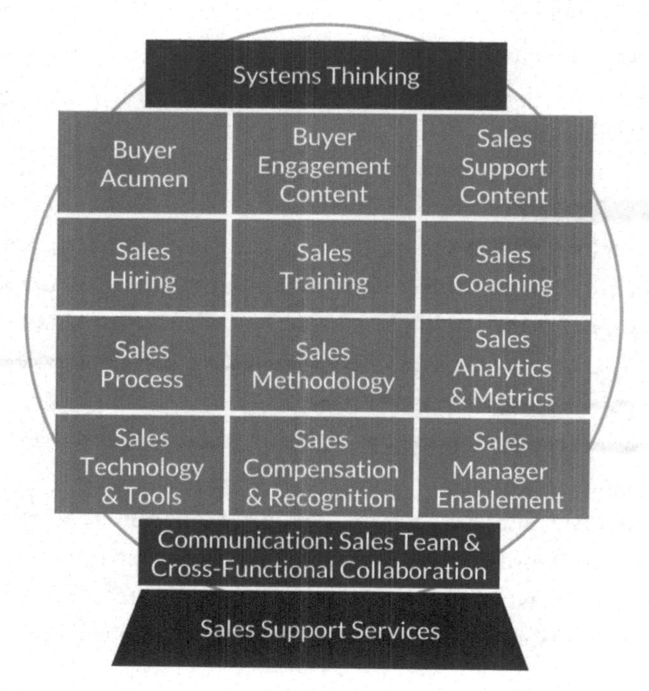

- **Sales coaching:** This is a known performance enhancer. You select a sales coaching model and implement a competency development framework, remove obstacles, enable managers, and engage reps and managers in an ongoing process to identify and close sales competency gaps to increase organizational sales mastery and performance.
- **Sales process:** In this building block, you work with others to align your sales process to the buying process, and document the process objectives, tasks, and exit criteria for buyers and sellers in each stage.
- **Sales methodology:** In this building block, you collaborate to select appropriate sales methodologies for prospecting, opportunity management, and strategic account management. You work to develop sales competencies by role, from a top-producer analysis whenever possible or proven best practices.
- **Sales analytics and metrics:** Here you benchmark your sales metrics, such as conversion ratios, average sales price, cross-sell, ramp-up times for onboarding, sales velocity, sales productivity, quota attainment, content sharing, or key performance indicators (KPIs)—whatever is important for your business. You collaborate to track results pre- and post-training as well as following your sales onboarding and learning metrics, which will allow you to analyze everything. Using whatever tools are available, you can analyze customers, territories, purchase patterns, and more to understand your business and improve performance.
- **Sales technology and tools:** Here, you work with others to select and implement sales technology to support your sales force, create efficiency, increase time spent selling, and support sales effectiveness.
- **Sales compensation and recognition:** In this building block, you collaborate to ensure you have sales compensation, incentive, recognition, and reward plans that encourage the behaviors your senior leaders expect and the results they want.
- **Sales manager enablement:** This is deep enough to be a separate book, but it must be included in any sensible sales enablement plan. Here, you train managers to support their reps in achieving their quota, including how to analyze performance, select appropriate interventions, and coach effectively. You develop a coaching culture and implement a framework for sales competency development. You also determine your sales management operating system and the management disciplines

you want to instill, train managers on them, and hold them accountable for executing your cadence.

The building blocks are supported by communication (both being the point-of-contact for communication to the sales team and fostering cross-functional communication and collaboration) and systems thinking.

Lastly, as applicable and desired, you can choose to provide a variety of sales support services, which includes things like coaching services, RFP support, and research support, often using a services level agreement (SLA) with the sales force.

In the following chapters I detail each building block, giving you the information you need to implement them effectively to start or evolve your sales enablement function and achieve the business results you and your executive team want. But first, we need to address systems thinking.

What Is Systems Thinking?

Daniel H. Kim, author of numerous books on systems thinking and co-founder of Pegasus Communications and the MIT Center for Organizational Learning, offers the following definition for systems thinking: "A system is any group of interacting, interrelated, or interdependent parts that form a complex and unified whole that has a specific purpose."

He continues: "The key thing to remember is that all of the parts are interrelated and interdependent in some way. Without such interdependencies, we have just a collection of parts, not a system."

Let's think about this in a different way. A car, for example, has many systems that work together so that it runs smoothly. These major systems include the engine, fuel system, exhaust system, cooling system, lubrication system, electrical system, transmission, and the chassis. Further, the chassis includes the wheels and tires, the brakes, the suspension system, and the body. If there's a problem with the drive train, the electrical system (such as the starter, battery, or alternator), or if several of the cylinders aren't firing (a fuel system problem), the car won't run very well.

The human body has systems too. Each system—respiratory, cardiovascular, pulmonary, skeletal, endocrine, or digestive—plays its part in a healthy, well-functioning body.

It's the same in an organization.

Some systems exist externally, like the political environment, socioeconomic conditions, and micro- and macroeconomic factors. Others are internal to the organization. I like to focus on internal systems and figure out the moving parts to make sure they're not only healthy independently, but also working well together. Systems occur at the organizational, functional (department), position (role), and task levels. Of the many possible organizational systems, I've found that four produce the best results:

- The Sales Hiring System
- The Sales Readiness System
- The Sales Training System
- The Sales Management System

I haven't always called those systems by these names. Before "sales readiness" was a common term, I called that system "sales support." The Sales Training System is technically a subset of readiness, but it's important enough with enough moving parts to call it out separately; it also includes a subsystem, which is the 5 Stages of Sales Mastery and Behavior Change.

Every system has a purpose, and for systems to produce the best results, all parts must be present and functioning at optimal levels. We have an opportunity to use critical thinking to analyze the relationships between each part of our organizational system to understand them more fully and make better decisions about how to improve business outcomes.

Summary

In this chapter I introduced the 12 building blocks, describing each one and how they fit together as a whole. But it's also important to recognize at this stage that you can use the building blocks as your situation allows and dictates; that is, they are by no means suggested as sequential steps. This will become clearer in the following chapters, and you will be able to better see which blocks require your attention.

I also showed how I use systems thinking to create interdependencies, and how the four sales systems I use—hiring, readiness, training, and management—support the building blocks and create cross-functional collaboration.

We're now ready to discuss the first building block, buyer acumen.

2

Buyer Acumen

The shift to a buyer-centric perspective is long overdue in the sales profession. The concept certainly isn't new. Thought leaders and progressive sales professionals have been implementing it for years. Unfortunately, it's far from pervasive. Over the past several years, B2B buying research has consistently indicated buyers' dissatisfaction with seller behavior.

As sales enablers, if our role is to guide our sales forces to higher levels of sales effectiveness, this is a crucial building block. I call this deeper understanding of our market and buyers "buyer acumen." While it's helpful to include perspectives from marketing and your front-line sellers and managers, your personas should not be created solely from an inside-out perspective. Instead, it's best to base this acumen and your personas on market research and discussions with your real buyers or others like them. If you don't have the internal expertise to conduct the necessary market research, you should hire someone who does.

Personas With Roles and Goals and Defining COIN-OP

There are more in-depth perspectives elsewhere about the different approaches to building buyer personas (I've learned the most from the work of Tony Zambito and Adele Revella), but I'll provide some guidance here. Useful personas include so much more than a simple profile of your buyers, but that concept helps most people grasp what a persona is.

As opposed to the ideal customer profile (ICP), which is a profile of the company, a buyer persona is a detailed description of your target buyers for each role that is typically involved in the purchase of your company's products and services.

Here are the things to consider as you research and build your personas.

- Roles and Goals:
    - Who are your buyers? Who are the decision makers, influencers, and stakeholders who typically buy from you? (In other words, who participates in the customer buying committee and purchase process for your products and services?)
    - What are their roles, titles, and responsibilities?

Relative to your solutions and the problems you solve, let's use my acronym COIN-OP, which represents the challenges, opportunities, impacts, needs, outcomes, and priorities that matter most to your buyers:

- **C/O:** What challenges do they face or what opportunities might they capitalize on?
- **I:** What are the risks and impacts of the status quo? What happens if they fail to address the challenges or capitalize on the opportunities?
- **N:** Based on these assessments, what are their needs and wants (relative to the problems you can solve)?
- **O/P:** Because of the **COIN**, what are the outcomes they've set (or should set), and how do they prioritize their needs and desired outcomes? What are the upsides for them if they do succeed?

Here are some other factors you might include:

- **Metrics:** How are they measured? What are the metrics that matter most to them, and how do they define success in their role?
- **Budgets:** What are their typical budgets, spans of control, and purchasing authority?
- **Buying process:** What is the typical buyer's journey? Who do they interact with internally during it? What are the most common decision criteria? How do buyers make their decisions?
- **Company:** In what size company or verticals do they typically work? (This is where you'd use the ICP info, which is more useful for targeting than understanding.)
- **Other pressures:** What other risks, pressures, or internal politics might influence your buyers?
- **Personal factors:** What emotional factors or personal needs might be in play?

It's helpful to think of personas as people, but it's also important to remember the difference between the two. Personas provide useful intelligence based on research and data for guiding your marketing efforts and preparing sales reps to approach buyers they don't know yet. However, they're still just generalizations. While marketing is evolving thanks to targeting methods and account-based marketing (ABM), it generally remains a "one-to-many" approach; sales is still a "one-to-one" or "one-to-a-few" activity. When selling, you should maximize your persona data initially, but then work to get beyond the persona research to more in-depth knowledge about the real people with whom you're working.

The decision criteria for a specific buyer, for example, could be very close to what the persona research indicates, but as a sales professional working with other humans, you need to get to the nitty-gritty of their challenges, opportunities, impacts, needs, outcomes, and priorities, as well as risks, metrics, pressures, politics, emotional factors, personal needs, and the individualized situational assessment for the real people making the buying decisions.

Buyer acumen gives reps the foundation to prove their interest in your buyers and demonstrate your deep understanding of their situation. B2B buying research continually points to the customer's desire to feel understood (and, unfortunately, how buyers think that the average sales reps fall short in this regard). Demonstrating this understanding and personalizing your messaging and sales conversations accordingly is a vital tenet of credibility and trust, especially when reps do so without discussing a solution until they fully understand the problem. (This is why I consider patience to be a selling superpower.)

Buying Process and Exit Criteria

"Exit criteria" is a term from Six Sigma that refers to the things you need to complete in a process stage before moving forward. Thus, buying process exit criteria are the things each buyer needs to see, hear, feel, understand, and believe in each stage of their purchase pursuit before they'll be comfortable moving forward with you. Knowing this, you can expand your research to include a typical buying process and the buying process exit criteria for each persona. It's also an opportunity to align your sales process to the buying process, which we'll discuss in the sales process building block (chapter 8).

So, how do you determine how your buyers make purchase decisions? Think about these questions:

- Who do they typically collaborate with internally as they make purchase decisions for products and services like yours?
- If they have a defined process, what is it? I prefer to document the entire customer lifecycle (which includes the buying process), but at a minimum, start with the buying process.
- What are their overall decision criteria, and what are their buying process exit criteria at each stage of the process?

Once you know the buying journey that most of your prospects traverse, you can align your sales process to support it. I don't mean to minimize the other aspects of process alignment (this is important work and often missing or done poorly with an inside-out perspective rather than outside-in), but I tend to place the most emphasis on preparing to support the buying process exit criteria for your buyers.

This is the central task in opportunity management and a key lever for performance improvement. If you understand your buyer's exit criteria for every process stage, it removes "selling by superstition" (Figure 2-1). It allows reps to focus on precisely what matters, delivering what the buyer needs and wants, when they need and want it.

Just as with personas, exit criteria can be documented generally, but when selling, they must be discovered and understood for each real buyer on the decision team. While I don't always refer to this as "qualification," it is an ongoing form of it. It's an understanding of the detailed criteria in each stage for each

Figure 2-1. Creating a Laser Focus on Buying Process Exit Criteria

Buying Process Exit Criteria

- Uncover
- Clarify
- Deliver
- Confirm

		The Buying Process				
		Identify Possible Initiatives	Research & Compare Solutions	Compare Options & Select a Solution	Negotiate & Finalize Terms	Make Purchase
Customer Life Cycle	Objectives					
	Tasks					
	Exit Criteria					

Selling by Superstition

1

2

Buying process exit criteria: What each decision maker needs to see, hear, feel, understand, and believe, in each stage of their buying process or purchase decision, to be comfortable moving forward to the next stage with you.

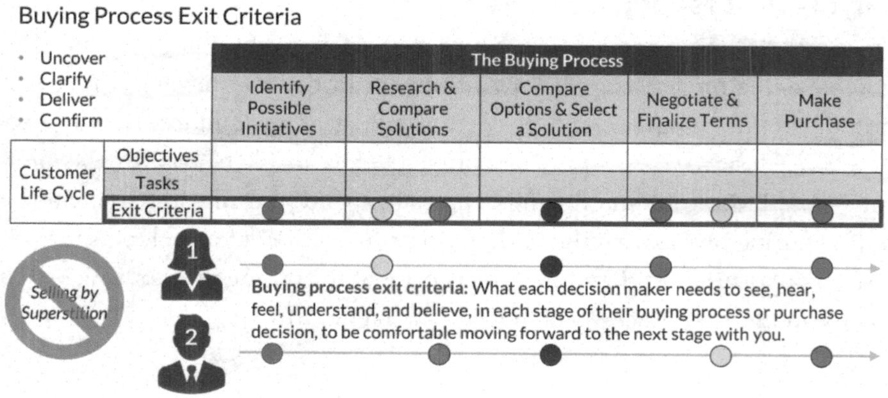

buyer. If you can't meet these criteria, it dramatically reduces your chance of winning the opportunity. While there are many qualification methods available, you must include this to reach maximum effectiveness.

For the best results, prepare your sales reps to intentionally uncover, clarify, meet, and confirm acceptance of the exit criteria for every buyer and in each stage of the buying process. This approach eliminates selling by superstition, where reps sell the same way to every buyer, regardless of differences in process or exit criteria.

This also brings a connection to sales messaging and buyer engagement content. Your buyer engagement content plan and the sales messaging you develop for your reps to use should both be based on your buyer acumen research and the buying process exit criteria you uncover.

Reps need to learn how to personalize messaging effectively, based on the COIN-OP and exit criteria, for the real buyers they are working with. Getting multiple buyers involved in a purchase and creating messaging that is appropriate to them is often called "multi-threading." I like to refer to it as "multilingual selling." I don't mean selling in French, German, Spanish, or Italian—I mean creating messaging that is selling effectively to CFOs, COOs, heads of marketing, or whomever your personas may be. Your reps need to speak the language of your buyers.

Some other things to consider:

- A buying process may not be linear. Different decision makers may be in different stages at different times; reps need to shepherd their buyers appropriately.
- Remember that outcomes and exit criteria may vary by buyer. Some exit criteria will be similar or the same, while some decision makers will have exit criteria unique to their role or personal perspective.
- New entrants (decision makers, influencers, or stakeholders), desired outcomes, or exit criteria can change things. Reps must pay attention and adapt accordingly.

People Acumen and Personal Needs

People acumen and personal needs are about paying attention and responding appropriately to what matters to each individual buyer. What are your buyers' primary needs or motivators? Combining the ideas of David McClelland, Abraham Maslow, Charles Handy, and more recently, Dan Pink, I've started to use this list of personal needs and motivators in my work. (If you like this list, here's a mnemonic to help you remember: PAM Orders Power BARS.) The elements are:

- Purpose
- Autonomy
- Mastery
- Order
- Power
- Belonging
- Achievement
- Recognition
- Safety

Sometimes there are blends. For example, some people with safety needs also crave order or belonging. Some with power needs crave autonomy or achievement.

As much as possible, take your buyers' personal needs and motivators into consideration when diagnosing needs and messaging solutions. You don't need to become an amateur psychologist to do this. Nor do you need your buyers to take validated psychometric assessments. Just do your best by asking questions, listening to answers, and observing, as well as summarizing and ensuring good communication, while comparing their answers with the list of personal needs. (In other words, do what you should already be doing!) And remember, this isn't an exact science and, frankly, it doesn't need to be.

It also helps to peel the onion or drill down rather than accept surface answers to questions as you work to understand what is important to your buyers and why. This will generally provide enough cues and clues to help you position and personalize your solution messaging for each buyer.

Summary

This chapter covers the crucial first building block, buyer acumen. First we defined buyer personas and described how they're built from market research but may include the perspectives of your sellers and managers. Understanding and appreciating your buyers by creating personas is the basis for generating personalized messaging throughout the buying process and understanding and documenting the exit criteria. Once you understand your prospects' buying journey, you can align your sales process to support and document it accordingly. This leads us to how to use buyer content, which is the subject of the next chapter and building block.

3

Buyer Engagement Content

As I described in chapter 1, there are two types of buyer engagement content:

- **Prospecting:** Similar to marketing content, this is designed by marketing for use by sales reps. It is what sales reps use when doing outreach to create awareness, generate buyer interest, and elicit a response.
- **Opportunity management:** This is designed to meet the buying process exit criteria for your typical buyer personas as they progress through their buying process and your sales process. This collateral engages buyers by answering their questions and clarifying your company, products, and services to so they can make effective buying decisions.

Content types may include:

- Blog posts
- Podcasts
- Self-assessments
- Customer testimonials
- Checklists
- How-to videos
- E-books
- Social media posts
- Industry or analyst reports
- Diagnostic tools
- Third-party perspectives
- Infographics
- Explainer videos
- Tip sheets
- Interviews
- Live or online demos
- Ratings websites
- Whitepapers
- Interactive tools
- Kits or tools
- Educational webinars

Buyer engagement content should build on your buyer acumen and your persona research, especially the buying process exit criteria by process stage, per persona.

Content creation is an excellent opportunity for you to collaborate with marketing, product marketing, and demand generation (or whatever versions of those functions exist in your company). Just remember how important buyer acumen is, as well as the foundational buyer persona research that fuels it. Don't make the common mistake of creating content based solely on internal opinions, even if those opinions are sourced from or include those of your sales force. Many marketing studies report that only a small percentage of marketing content is actually used by sellers. There are many reasons for this, some of which may be on the seller side, but a bigger issue is that the content doesn't really matter to the buyers because it doesn't satisfy their exit criteria.

What you learn about your buyers from this research can fuel your content marketing plan, demand generation approach, and sales prospecting plans, as well as your account executive's content strategy during opportunity management. When we understand the difference between the persona-level and the more detailed person-level, it becomes clear that we also need to provide a way for sales reps to personalize this content based on the differences they uncover between the generalized criteria from the research and the very specific criteria of the decision makers in a specific opportunity.

In fact, content research and creation are outstanding ways to build a buyer engagement content strategy. Sellers need to uncover and clarify exit criteria by buyer per stage, deliver whatever is required to satisfy the exit criteria, and confirm with each buyer that they have accepted your information and their exit criteria have been met. Marketing can create content based on buyer persona research to aid sellers with this.

In addition, sales reps should be able to customize the content's messaging, as appropriate, based on the real concerns and requirements of individual decision makers. The columns across the top of Table 3-1 represent the stages of a buying process. The top row, Buyer Role 1, includes the exit criteria for the first buyer persona. The second row, Content Plan, offers examples of the type of buyer engagement content you could create to satisfy the exit criteria.

This is the best way to develop a content plan to engage buyers throughout their process and meet their decision and exit criteria. The plan addresses the exit criteria using the type of content and media that makes sense for each case.

Table 3-1. Using Buying Process Exit Criteria to Create Buyer Engagement Content Plans

Buyer Persona	Interest	Qualify	Discovery	Solution Design	Proposal	Negotiate
Buyer Role 1	• Exit criteria • Exit criteria • Exit criteria	• Exit criteria	• Exit criteria • Exit criteria • Exit criteria	• Exit criteria • Exit criteria • Exit criteria • Exit criteria	• Exit criteria • Exit criteria	• Exit criteria
Content Plan	• Videos • Website pages • Blog posts • E-books • Testimonials	• Case studies • Business case forms	• Discovery summary template	• Brochures • Videos • Whitepapers • Tech specs • Endorsements	• References • ROI calculator • Proposal format	• N/A

Personas may have similar and unique exit criteria in each stage of their buying process. The messaging in the content should speak to your personas—for example, financial messaging for executive and financial buyers, technical information and workflow for feasibility and functional buyers, and messaging about risk management for the risk averse.

To understand and maximize your buyer engagement content, it's important to know how it is being used by your sellers and consumed by your buyers. Sales enablement software can help you do this. It's the sales content management or sales asset management category of software that does this. It can integrate with your CRM, serve up the content at the right time to your reps, and track consumption with your buyers. With enough data, you can even begin to correlate the use and consumption of the content by buyer type and stage with a higher likelihood of moving forward through your process milestones.

Summary

Now you can see the foundational importance of buyer acumen and persona research to deliver relevant, personalized buyer engagement content. As you develop a buyer engagement content strategy, you'll continue to customize your messaging based on the differences you find between researched personas and real decision makers. In the next building block, we consider how sales support content fits into our overall content strategy.

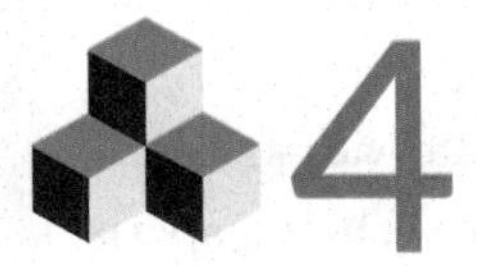

4 Sales Support Content

Sales support content is what supports your sales force while they are selling as your leadership team intends—that is, following your sales process and using your sales methodology. Sales support content includes:

- Performance support
- Sales playbooks
- Materials
- Tools
- Workflow performance support software

When sales support is delivered digitally or through software, this category blurs with the building block for sales technology and tools. In this case, the software enables the use of the content, but the content itself (which is usually the sales methodology or how you want your reps to sell) is the sales support content.

The difference between performance support and workflow performance support is simple:

- Performance support consists of paper or digital job aids or "cheat sheets" that help reps complete a task, such as preparing a prospecting approach, responding to a buyer's concern, or completing an account plan.
- Workflow performance support adds the aspect of timing by introducing the content to the rep at the right time in their process

and reminding them of the need to do it, or how to do it. This is often referred to as prescriptive selling or guided selling.

Let's look closer at the different types of sales support content.

Performance Support

Performance support tools are sometimes referred to as job aids, cheat sheets, or worksheets.

If you're creating performance support materials, collaborate with someone who is an expert in instructional design, unless you already are. These experts often work in your training or L&D department. If this function reports to you, hire an expert or contract with a freelancer or consultant.

In either case, don't overcomplicate your performance support materials. Stay focused on supporting the rep as they are doing the job at hand, as it was taught. The purpose of performance support isn't to reteach the content; it's to offer reminders and provide a form or guide to help the reps more easily complete the task at a higher level of accuracy or competency than they might have without the aid.

Sales Playbooks

Sales playbooks contain all the pieces that make up your company's go-to-market approach. They can be paper, digital, standalone, or integrated. Playbooks often include:

- Target market information
- Buyer personas and ideal customer profiles
- Company information
- Product information and pricing
- Sales processes and workflows with standard operating procedures
- CRM guidance
- Sales call planning templates
- Sales content management (such as case studies or testimonials)
- Multi-touch cadences with sales messaging (such as sample emails, call scripts, voicemail scripts, or social approaches)
- A discovery guide
- Your qualification methodology
- Demo or presentation advice
- Competitive intelligence

- Proposal guidelines and templates
- Negotiation advice

Whenever possible, use digital playbooks that integrate into your organization's CRM to support your sales process. This will support your sales reps' daily workflow.

Materials

Materials serve to remind salespeople about training content, and include things such as learning reinforcement and virtual coaching activities. This content might include quizzes, glossaries, short videos, exercises, activities, or role-play guides.

Tools

Tools support training content or sales methodology. They're similar to job aids but are often digital and interactive. Examples include an ROI calculator and scheduling software. Tools usually have a singular focus and support one activity or task.

Workflow Performance Support Software

Rather than being a basic tool, workflow performance support software is full-blown software that helps reps implement what they were taught and what they are expected to do as they are working (for example, using your prescribed sales methodology in their sales process workflow).

If a digital playbook is automated or integrated into the CRM, it is a version of workflow performance support. The SaaS product, WalkMe, can provide guidance on how to use a software program from inside the program. Guided selling software like Altify, Membrain, Revegy, ringDNA, Revenue Grid, and Pega can guide reps in doing their jobs, such as managing territories, building a relationship map, prospecting, managing opportunities, or planning and executing account plans.

Summary

The purpose of sales support content is to aid and improve performance of sales reps, not reteach them. In the form of expertly crafted job aids, worksheets, sales playbooks, and the like, sales support content can guide your reps with well-placed just-in-time reminders. Now it's time to select your sales team—building block 4 and building block 5.

5

Sales Hiring

The Sales hiring block and my sales hiring system are synonymous, so in this chapter I describe them together.

The Sales Hiring System

Can you pick your next sales team (sellers, managers, and leaders) or individual sales hire, and get it right? What percentage of the time?

Your Sales Hiring System is the foundation on which everything else is built. As Jim Collins famously said in his book *Good to Great*, "Get the right people on the bus, the wrong people off the bus, and the right people in the right seats."

Systems are powerful. They help you maximize the potential of your talent. In fact, great systems can help you get above-average performance from otherwise average players, which is why I build systems. I'm fond of quoting the late Geary Rummler: "If you pit a good performer against a bad system, the system will win almost every time."

So, a bad system may hinder even your best performers. If you don't have the right players in the right roles, the building blocks and other systems simply won't produce the maximum possible results. This is much like the nature versus nurture debate in psychology. So, rather than betting on nature *or* nurture, we're going to fine-tune both as much as possible.

Using the right building blocks with any one system will do something for you, and when you can combine them the effects will compound. But you can't overcompensate for a lack of appropriate talent. This is especially true in the sales profession. B2B professional sellers are like the Olympic athletes of the corporate world, the astronauts of business, or the Navy Seals of sales. They need to have "the right stuff," or what my friends at the Objective Management Group call the "will to sell" and the "right sales DNA."

If you want to improve your sales onboarding and decrease ramp-up time while increasing average new-hire production, the first step of effective sales onboarding is to hire the right talent for the right roles. Then, you also want to put them into the right culture, environment, and system.

If you want to increase the performance of one sales team, there are many things you can do, but the single biggest step may be to put the right manager in place (hiring and promoting sales managers effectively).

We all know this, right? Heads nod around conference room tables whenever I say this. So here's the big question: If we all know this, why don't put more energy into selecting the right talent?!?

I'm a little passionate about this—I've witnessed the massive impact talent can make. I've seen how the right manager can reduce first-year, new-hire churn from 75 to 25 percent. I've seen a team with solid B players, but no hardcore A players, double their average monthly production in six months after the right (replacement) sales manager joined the team. Of course, other factors and initiatives were in play in both examples, but they wouldn't have worked as well without the right talent.

And conversely, twice in my career, I've witnessed reputable, well-qualified, highly experienced vendors do complete talent audits of the sales force (reps and managers), with approved job profiles, competency measurements, psychometric assessments, and calibrated reporting. Company leaders were engaged throughout the process and signed off on each step. Everyone was educated about how the process and tools worked and what they would tell us. But when the final reports rolled in, senior leaders didn't like what they said about the limited capability of the current sales force, so they put the reports on a shelf because they were either overwhelmed or in disbelief. Do you think sales results improved? Sadly, in *both* cases the organizations missed quotas repeatedly and by large margins and layoffs occurred a few quarters later.

SOURCING AND RECRUITING

When you fix your hiring process, you might also expose problems with sourcing and recruiting. I once developed a highly effective selection system for a B2B financial services firm, but we ran into a roadblock shortly after implementation. After we developed the ideal profile, there wasn't a single candidate in the pipeline who was remotely close to qualifying!

Keep in mind that few candidates will be an exact match—people are, well, human. There's a give and take in hiring. If the person can learn, is willing to learn, and will accept coaching, you can teach them new skills. You need to be a bit more selective with traits, but you can also allow some shortfalls if you can compensate for them in other ways, such as through coaching or additional kinds of support.

In this case, now that we had learned to hire right, we needed to source right for the new hiring profile. For that, we worked very closely with recruiting and HR to figure things out. That was a great learning experience.

For those of you who are now clapping, laughing, or crying, and want to do something differently, there's a better way to approach sales hiring. Use a Sales Hiring System (Figure 4-1). While any of the elements of a system can improve your hiring approach, the combination of system elements working together is powerful.

Hiring right is essential, and mistakes are costly in a variety of ways. Get consultant advice if you need it. In some companies, especially where each hire was critical, I have implemented every element in this system. In others, I selected

Figure 4-1. The Sales Hiring System

the combination of elements that made the most sense for the company and culture. In every case, I included assessments and behavioral interviews. And, unless I couldn't sell it internally, I also implemented role plays and simulations to validate skills.

Elements of a Sales Hiring System

This system is a framework to develop a hiring process, not the process itself. The framework will help you choose and build the elements of a Sales Hiring System that is right for your company. The lighter color elements in the figure are things you do behind the scenes. The darker colored boxes represent things you will eventually do with your candidates.

Determine Sales Competencies

The first step is to determine the competencies (skills and behaviors) needed for sales success in your company for each role. There will be overlap between roles and other things, but list them all and create a library from which to pull. This is the foundation for everything else in this system. For your reference, there are experts and resources who can help you with this process:

- ATD's World-Class Sales Competency Model
- Sales consulting firms like Sales Benchmark Index, Alexander Group, and ZS Associates
- Most management consulting firms
- Dave Brock has an excellent starter kit that (if asked) he shares for free
- Cheryl Lasse of SkillDirector can help you build a competency model and assess skill levels over time (and tie training courses to them to automatically build personalized learning plans). She has a rapid competency development process that produces a competency model in a few weeks. She also has a great online tool you can explore for delivering and managing competency assessments.
- Some assessment vendors also use competency-based approaches and can help you select competencies by role, which their assessments will then support. At SPARXiQ, we partner with Dave Kurlan's Objective Management Group to offer both individual and organizational assessments that examine 21 proven sales competencies and highlight strengths, developmental areas, and gaps to close to improve sales force performance.

- At SPARXiQ we also have a competency model that sits behind our Modern Sales Foundations course.

There are plenty of other competency experts out there. Even some sales training firms do this work.

Determine Traits

Once the competencies are in place, you'll determine the traits (also known as attributes or characteristics, personality, or mindsets) required to support the competencies and thrive in the various roles. (In addition to high skill levels, selling requires certain mindsets and traits. It's more like being an Olympic athlete than an accountant.) These may also vary by role. Create a traits library, similar to the one you created for your competencies.

Create Job Documentation

For each sales role, create a job description, job specifications, and a job profile. Make sure to document the tasks required for success and slot in the competencies and traits you defined to build the requirements for each role.

Select Psychometric Assessments

In this step, the key is to find statistically validated psychometric assessments that can assess the competencies and traits that are vital for your sales hires to possess.

Approaches vary, but in the past, I preferred assessing and profiling the top producers inside a company so that I could find more like them, rather than assessing against a stock "sales profile." I did this by looking at the top, bottom, and middle performers to find statistically valid differences between top and middle performers and the top and bottom. This helps you determine which patterns to avoid as much as which patterns to seek out.

While I had successes with this method, there is a potential limitation—even the top producers inside your company may not have every characteristic that an elite, world-class sales performer possesses. It also takes a lot more time and expertise to rely on a top-producer analysis project that you (or someone you hire) must conduct. If you use a proven-effective sales assessment with a high degree of predictive validity, based on the profile of world-class, elite sales producers, you can fast-forward through much of that work.

This thinking also applies if you have a small sales force. In this case, you may not be able to do a valid analysis of your data and may need to rely more on the assessment company's experience until you build your data by hiring more and correlating to performance.

Some vendors sell their assessments as a "weed out" tool. Others will advise you that the assessment results should be weighted as a third of the decision process. I like to use the assessment to prioritize candidates for screening as well as inform the interview process and the final decision. This is especially helpful if you have a large number of resumes to screen. You might also weed out candidates based on how far they score outside your ideal profile, or if they score poorly on competencies or mindsets that are proven to be key differentiators.

Whatever you do, be consistent. Other than validity studies, that's what keeps it legal and ethical.

While I don't have a PhD in psychometrics, from the research I've done I strongly recommend normative assessments to ipsative assessments. Normative assessments allow you to compare the rep (the candidate being assessed or internal rep being evaluated) to others (hence the term *normed* or *normative*). Ipsative assessments tell you something about the person as an individual, from their perspective, but they can't be compared with others statistically. Normative assessments are legal for hiring as long as they're statistically validated, job-related, free from adverse impact to members of a protected group or minority, and meet the government's standards related to testing (as contained in the Uniform Guidelines on Employee Selection Procedures).

When evaluating assessments, look for those that are:

- Sales specific
- Customizable for industry, company, and role
- Normative versus ipsative
- Statistically validated in the recent past by a reliable and neutral third-party, including predictive validity for sales (the vendor should be willing to share this report, which is often referred to as a technical manual or research report)
- Compliant with government and legal regulations (which the vendor should also be able to share in their technical analysis)

Don't let perfect be the enemy of good; there is no perfect assessment. Demand validity studies. Any statistically validated approach (by a reliable, independent third party) will likely be far better than what you're doing today, especially if it's woven in with these other methods.

Implement Behavioral Interviewing

Behavioral interviewing is a well-established, effective, and very underutilized method for hiring. I've interviewed at companies where recruiters and hiring managers claimed to use a behavioral approach, but the interviewers asked me no (or very few) behavioral questions. You should establish behavioral interview questions to gauge whether candidates possess the competencies and traits you seek, and can provide examples of such from their past behaviors (past behavior is the best predictor of future behavior). Then, use the questions.

For a situation, task, action, result (STAR) framework:

- Ask the candidate to give you an example of a time when they ________ [fill in the blank with the behavior you want to assess].
- Then, through follow-up questions, guide them to provide:
  - The situation (which relates to the competency or trait you're assessing)
  - The task at hand
  - The action they took
  - The result they got
  - And, possibly, what they learned from it (this is a great follow-up closing question)

Here are a few example prompts:

- "Tell me about a time when you couldn't get a response from a key prospect, and what you finally did to break through and land a meeting with them."
- "You mentioned that you often work with multiple decision makers on your more complex opportunities. Can you share a time when you were working with multiple buyers in the same meeting, who had different interests and needs, and how you handled that meeting to get buy-in from each buyer to move forward?"
- "Tell me about a time when you were creating a plan for a key account in your territory. I'm especially interested in how you assessed the account's potential, set an account objective, and then developed a plan to achieve the objective."

Establish a way for interviewers to take notes and score answers, perhaps against a best-case response. If you use multiple interviewers, ensure you have trained them all well, and that you assemble them to share thoughts, calibrate their candidate ratings, and align (as much as possible) on the interview scores by competency. Yes, this is extra work. But given the cost of a bad sales hire, it's worth it.

Test Situational or Hypothetical Judgment

Situational judgment questions can help establish what candidates would do in difficult situations that they are likely to face when selling for your company. This can be especially helpful if they haven't faced the exact behavioral situation needed to answer a behavioral question. Establish some challenging hypothetical scenarios (built from real case studies at your company, usually from your top producers based on what they did) and prepare questions and best-case responses to assess candidates' answers.

For example, you could ask:

- "Imagine that you're in a conference room with key executives from an important client. Each one has different decision criteria for selecting your product. How do you handle that in a group meeting?"
- "What would you do if your primary contact at your largest account—which is responsible for 60 percent of your territory revenue and 12 percent of your company's revenue—told you that a new senior executive joined the company, and they were weighing whether they should continue to source a product solely from your company or reduce risk by purchasing from multiple suppliers?"

Orchestrate Skill Validation

Would you hire a musician without hearing them play? An actor or dancer without an audition? How about a basketball player without seeing them play? Of course not.

Since we can't observe sales reps from other companies the same way we can audition musicians, actors, and dancers, or scout basketball players, you have to orchestrate other ways to validate their skills and "see them in action." One option is to create role-play scenarios or simulations (sims) to verify that a candidate can demonstrate the skills they tell you they have. Sims can be low-tech role plays (but please don't use "sell me this pen"!) or high-tech options with virtual coaching solutions, virtual role plays, or full-blown online, branched simulations with scoring. Your mileage may vary with these approaches, but role play works.

Are you hiring a sales development rep or field rep who will prospect? Have them email you and call you. Give them a real or simulated case study or prospect and see what they can do (but calling you, not the real prospect). Use your imagination, keeping the tasks and sims as realistic as possible, and see how candidates handle themselves.

The one thing most average sales reps can sell is themselves. The two things they can't fake their way past are an excellent assessment and a demonstration of the skills you expect. I've used these "auditions" to hire sales reps and sales trainers by having several finalists compete (although not in front of each other). You'd be surprised how many people falter at this stage.

Perform Background and Reference Checks

For finalists, conduct background checks, consistently following HR and federal and state legal guidelines, as well as your company's policies and approved practices. This might include employment, education, criminal background checks, and drug testing, as well as reference checks. Reference checks are now often less valuable than in the past because so many companies only identify the person's role, dates of employment, and compensation and will not comment on the employee or their performance due to legal concerns. At least run a criminal background check, where allowed by law. Seek guidance here from experts.

Putting It All Together

As you weave these elements (or the ones you choose) together, follow a structured, logical process. You need to:

- Pick the elements you will use in your hiring process.
- Determine your process flow. For example:
    - When will you use assessments? (I prefer upfront, before the first full interview.)
    - Will you use hypothetical questions to assess situational judgment? (I would.)
    - How will you conduct the skill validation role plays? (Involve the hiring manager.)
- Have a coordinated plan for conducting interviews. Considerations:
    - Will you assign competencies to the various interviewers (break up the interview), or will everyone conduct the full interview? (I think both work well.)

    - How will you calibrate ratings across interviewers to help the hiring manager understand the ratings and include them in their decision? (Without discussion and calibration, everyone's idea of a 3 or 4 rating may not be the same. Having a conversation about the finalist candidates and their interviews will be more helpful than looking at mathematical averages.)
- Determine how you will ensure compliance—consistency is critical for fairness and legality.
- Train hiring managers and interviewers and implement your system and measure results.

Summary

As this chapter on establishing a sales hiring process shows, the combinations of techniques and scenarios are too numerous to mention, but these are the sorts of things you need to think through. An experienced consultant or vendor partner can help you establish a flow and process for hiring. While putting this type of selection system in place seems daunting, it's the research, project work, decisions, and implementation of a new process that are the hard part. Once you have established the elements with a sensible process and people are trained on how to use the system, you'll build momentum quickly, as people see it working.

When you consider how critical it is to have the right sales talent, and the costs of turnover, failed reps, and the opportunity loss of barely successful reps that consistently miss quota, you'll be glad you invested the time and energy to hire right. Now you're ready for the sales training building block.

6

Sales Training

Sales training is a significant aspect of sales enablement. There is a battle cry among some in the profession recently that "Sales enablement is not just training!" That is true; so at the start of this chapter, I want to be clear about a few things:

- Yes, sales enablement is not *just* training, as I hope the broad nature of the building blocks shows.
- The importance of this collaboration with other functions will be evident as we progress through this building block and look closely at *what* we are training.

That said, I also am not going to downplay the importance of training nor the transformative power of this building block. Teaching your sales force how to get the best possible results and guiding them through the implementation to reach sales mastery is a crucial tenet of enablement, and we can't downplay it if we want to improve sales performance. In fact, many of the other functions provide inputs into the training.

This building block is supported by two of the four systems we'll discuss in this book, the Sales Readiness System and the Sales Training System. (And since coaching is part of the training system, technically, it's also supported by the Sales Management System.)

I've been rightly accused of being a "nester" because I've designed the Sales Training System to be nested in the Sales Readiness System, and the 5 Stages of Sales Mastery and Behavior Change to be nested within the Sales Training System. Once I explain these systems and subsystems, I think you'll see this as very natural and organic, especially since the concept of systems is that everything is connected as part of a larger ecosystem. The whole is greater than the sum of its parts.

The Sales Readiness System

Let's begin with an overview of the Sales Readiness System, since the training system is embedded in it (Figure 6-1).

The Sales Readiness System consists of these steps:

- Ensure deep market and buyer persona knowledge.
- Document the buying process with decision and exit criteria.
- Create buyer engagement content that aligns with decision and exit criteria.
- Ensure reps have the domain and business acumen, with solution acumen, to communicate value in your buyers' language.
- Align the sales process to the buying process and use a buyer-oriented, consultative, solution-focused, and outcome-driven sales methodology.
- Use sales enablement tools to manage, share, and track content and improve sales efficiency and effectiveness.

Figure 6-1. The Sales Readiness System

- Use analytics to track training, content, sales behavior, and outcomes.
- Train reps to engage buyers in valuable business conversations and create real value and differentiation through their buyer acumen, domain and business acumen, and solution acumen.

My good friend Jim Ninivaggi was both a sales readiness expert and evangelist. He once wrote that sales readiness "involves assessing and certifying whether salespeople are equipped with the proper skills and knowledge to have the conversations needed throughout a buyer's journey. Training and coaching play an important role in creating a productive, knowledgeable, agile, and ready sales force."

In my experience, the effectiveness of sales readiness activity is determined by the ingredients and the execution. Especially in today's B2B marketplace, we must prepare sellers with more in-depth knowledge about business in general as well as the buyers they serve. Since there is a separate Sales Training System to guide execution, we will focus on the elements for the Sales Readiness System.

Buyer Personas

This element helps ensure your reps understand the market you serve and the buyer personas who purchase what you sell. I cover this in more detail in the chapter on buyer acumen.

Buying Process and Exit Criteria

As described earlier, buying process exit criteria are what each buyer needs to see, hear, feel, understand, and believe in each stage of their purchase pursuit, to feel comfortable moving forward to the next step or stage with you. In the readiness system, the persona and buying process lay the foundation for what matters most to your buyers. Without deeply understanding the market and their buyers, salespeople cannot maximize their potential (and will not be "readied" or enabled to sell).

Buyer Engagement Content Creation

In this element you can create a content marketing or buyer engagement content plan that aligns with the personas and exit criteria. Sales enablement leaders don't often own this step, but should collaborate cross-functionally with marketing and product marketing to build these plans and the resulting content to meet their buyers' requirements.

Exit criteria are like the needle and thread that weave through these first few components of the Sales Readiness System. If you know what buyers generally want to see, hear, feel, understand, and believe in each stage of their buying process, you can create marketing and sales collateral ("buyer engagement content") that are aimed at satisfying those needs and wants. I discuss this element more fully in chapter 3, "Buyer Engagement Content."

Domain Expertise and Business or Solution Acumen

This is where you train your sales reps to engage buyers in insightful, valuable business conversations. Domain expertise, business acumen, and solution acumen are essential inputs to an effective sales methodology. They provide a similar "needle and thread" action of sewing things together on this side of the Sales Readiness System, as you saw earlier on the buyer-focused side.

Domain expertise is an understanding of the vertical industries you serve, including the challenges, opportunities, technologies, regulations, legislation, business practices, current events or news, and the general state of the industry. To create real value and differentiation, and to conduct productive sales and business conversations—including discovery and, eventually, solution dialogues—reps must have the domain expertise and general business acumen to uncover problems that matter enough to solve, and the ability to discuss the value of solutions. Depending on the level of the buyers you work with, this may also include deep financial acumen.

Solution acumen includes the ability to:

- Select the right solution to the problem.
- Work with the buyer to co-create the solution or how it will be applied (fostering buy-in and ownership).
- Communicate the value of solutions by tying them to the resolution of challenges, risks, or opportunities and the attainment of the desired outcomes (again, reflected in the metrics that really matter).

Domain expertise, business and financial acumen, and solution acumen are becoming the ticket to entry to sell to executive buyers if you hope to:

- Earn credibility and trust.
- Ask the right questions to uncover problems that matter enough to solve (helping to avoid deal stalls and no-decision endings).
- Understand how buyers' challenges negatively impact the metrics that matter most to them and how your solution will positively impact those same metrics.

Sales Process and Methodology

In this element, you document and align processes and select a sales methodology that is modern, buyer centric, consultative, value focused, solution oriented, and outcome driven.

Sales process refers to the stages that an opportunity progresses through, from being a lead to where a purchase decision (or no decision) is made. You should record and align the stages of your sales process with the buying process, and document the following in each stage:

- Objectives
- Tasks (activities and steps)
- Exit criteria (what needs to be completed in the stage before moving forward)

The sales methodology, then, includes the buyer-facing tasks and activities that reps do in each stage. This is *what* the reps do to sell and *how* they do it. We'll talk more about these topics in the chapters on sales process and sales methodology, respectively.

Sales Enablement Technology

In this element, you can use available software to improve efficiency and sales effectiveness.

Years ago, before we even used the term *sales enablement*, a mentor of mine was fond of saying "technology is just an enabler." He was referring to e-learning technology at the time, but the sentiment remains true today and certainly applies equally to sales enablement technology. In 1995, he may also have been the first person I heard say that "a fool with a tool is still a fool," which I hear a lot today (and which also remains true). We'll cover this in more detail in the chapter on sales technology and tools.

Analytics

This is where we track training, content, sales behavior, and outcomes. We'll dive into this in the chapter on sales analytics and metrics.

The Sales Training System (a Subset of Sales Readiness)

This brings us to the Sales Training System (Figure 6-2). It's impossible to refer to sales readiness without including sales training, so the training system is part of the readiness system.

Figure 6-2. The Sales Training System

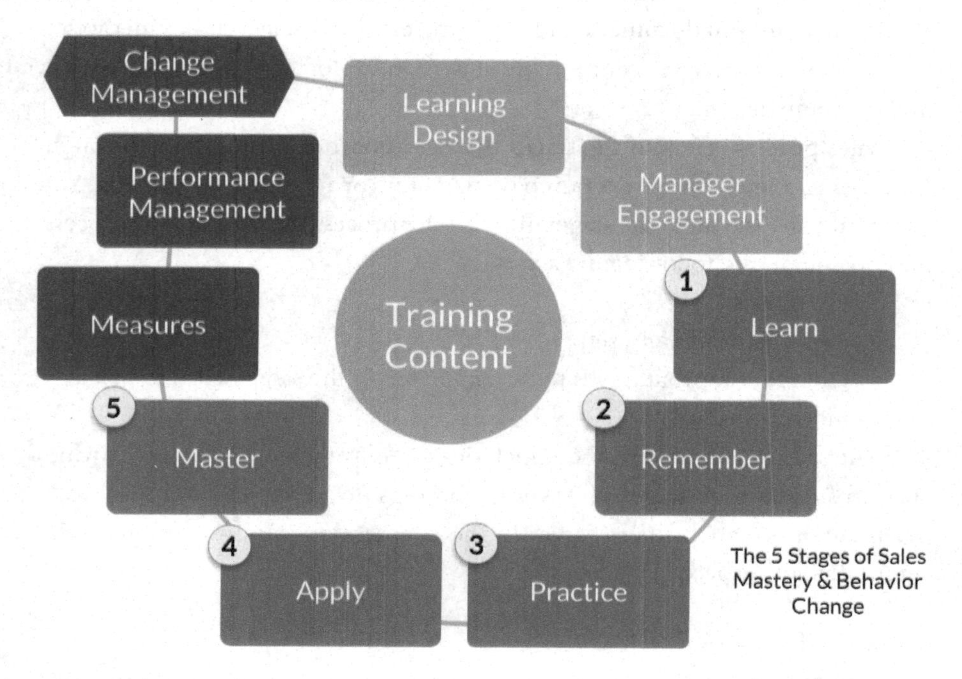

Even though it's part of the Sales Readiness System, the Sales Training System is important enough, and detailed enough, to deserve a full systemic treatment. In fact, it contains a subsystem of its own—the 5 Stages of Sales Mastery and Behavior Change.

Note that the Sales Training System components function as a change management system:

- Prepare for change:
  - Ensure that your training content will get results.
  - Design a great learning experience.
  - Engage, enable, and empower front-line sales managers.
- Guide the change (five stages):
  - Learn—train the content and validate learning occurred.
  - Remember—sustain the knowledge.
  - Practice—develop skills (practice with expert feedback loops).
  - Apply—transfer and apply skills on the job.
  - Master—coach to mastery over time.

- Cement the change:
    - Get metrics and measures in place.
    - Manage to behavior and performance expectations.
    - Lead and manage the change until it is cemented in the culture.

Let's examine the system components in detail.

Training Content

The best training or learning system in the world can't overcome poor content that won't produce real-world results. When training is the right solution, it all starts here. Training pros will be very familiar with needs and gap analysis, and I strongly encourage top producer analysis to find the differentiating practices between top sales producers and middle producers. Your content should be based on this, or (if you use a purchased sales methodology) at least customized to reflect the replicable practices of your top producers.

Learning Design

There is a big difference between presenting information and designing effective training. Much is written on the topic of instructional systems design, and there are many great resources that can help. These are my basic recommendations:

- Chunk, sequence, and layer the content and assess frequently.
- Separate knowledge and skill and blend the content, combining asynchronous learning (training the knowledge prerequisites using e-learning or other self-directed learning methods) with synchronous, virtual instructor-led training or classroom skills-based training (a flipped classroom with practice, feedback loops, and re-runs).
- Use as many simulations as possible to model the real world and show how knowledge and skills plug into process and workflow.
- Be sure to use evidence-based and performance-based instructional systems design or hire someone who does.

Manager Engagement

You should engage your front-line sales managers everywhere possible (based on the organizational tolerance for it, which will create natural limits). Sales managers are often made managers because they were the best salespeople, so they'll have excellent content feedback as subject matter experts and former top producers. Train them first. You need your managers to understand the content (in as much detail as the reps) and to know what their reps are learning. This allows you to develop their content buy-in to ensure they support it enthusiastically with their reps. For their part, managers must be able to diagnose performance issues and assess whether reps are using the best practices learned in training. And, finally, they must be prepared and enabled to train, sustain knowledge, help reps apply skills, and coach to mastery (the 5 Stages of Sales Mastery and Behavior Change; Figure 6-3).

In the training profession, the real-world application of what was learned in a training course is referred to as "training transfer," a concept that may be somewhat less familiar to sales enablement professionals, unless they come from a training background. How can you help sales reps use what you teach, on the job, with their buyers and customers?

- Reps need to learn the knowledge and skills you want them to use.
- Reps can't apply what they don't remember, so develop plans to reinforce content and improve retention—also known as knowledge sustainment. (Many tools use spaced repetition and gamification principles to assist with this.)
- We typically don't provide enough practice and feedback to help reps develop confidence and competence with the new skills. Whether it's through virtual practice and coaching tools, old-fashioned role plays, or other means, get your reps practicing in safe (but progressively challenging) learning settings with feedback loops (practice, feedback, re-do, feedback, re-do).
- Even if they remember what they learned and can do it, that doesn't mean reps will use what they've learned when they're selling. Develop plans for sales managers to follow up, help reps prepare to use their new skills on-the-job, and observe those skills in action. You can give managers "meetings in a box" (such as manager toolkits or manager implementation guides) to help them run meetings to reinforce concepts and get reps to prepare to use skills with real buyers. Performance support—such as forms, job aids, checklists, or other documents that help reps prepare to use the information—can help with this.
- Building training content into sales enablement applications and tools, electronic performance support systems, or CRM and process workflows makes excellent sense. Do everything you can to turn top-producer practices into "the way we do things around here."

Figure 6-3. The 5 Stages of Sales Mastery and Behavior Change

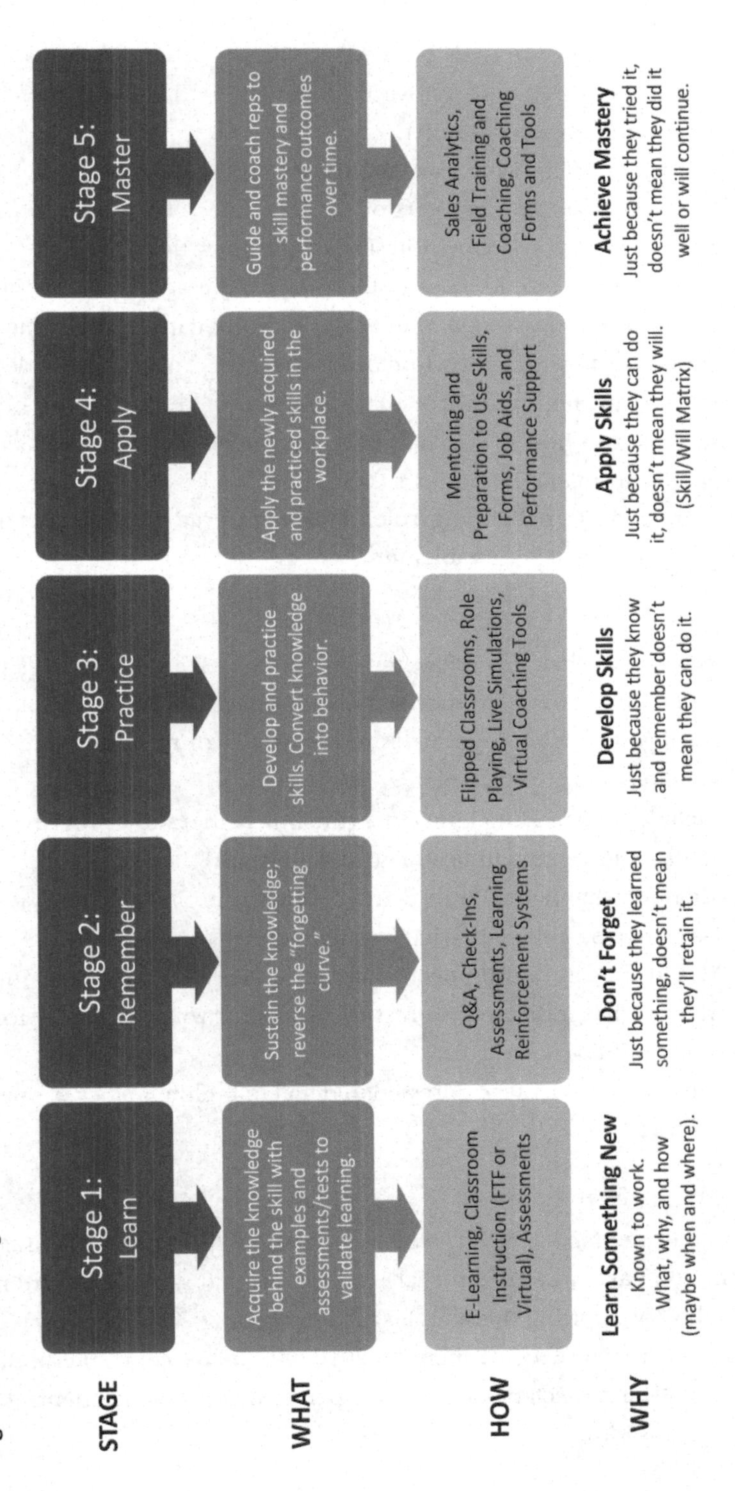

STAGE
WHAT
HOW
WHY
Stage 1: Learn
Acquire the knowledge behind the skill with examples and assesments/tests to validate learning.
E-Learning, Classroom Instruction (FTF or Virtual), Assessments
Learn Something New
Known to work.
What, why, and how (maybe when and where).
Stage 2: Remember
Sustain the knowledge; reverse the "forgetting curve."
Q&A, Check-Ins, Assessments, Learning Reinforcement Systems
Don't Forget
Just because they learned something, doesn't mean they'll retain it.
Stage 3: Practice
Develop and practice skills. Convert knowledge into behavior.
Flipped Classrooms, Role Playing, Live Simulations, Virtual Coaching Tools
Develop Skills
Just because they know and remember doesn't mean they can do it.
Stage 4: Apply
Apply the newly acquired and practiced skills in the workplace.
Mentoring and Preparation to Use Skills, Forms, Job Aids, and Performance Support
Apply Skills
Just because they can do it, doesn't mean they will. (Skill/Will Matrix)
Stage 5: Master
Guide and coach reps to skill mastery and performance outcomes over time.
Sales Analytics, Field Training and Coaching, Coaching Forms and Tools
Achieve Mastery
Just because they tried it, doesn't mean they did it well or will continue.

You'll notice the emphasis on feedback and coaching in the system. This should be no surprise—superlative evaluative and developmental coaching skills are required for sales excellence.

Coaching on using what was taught (activity) and how well the skills are being used (quality) are a key part of these transfer plans, but even after the skills have transferred, coaching will sustain and grow the skills.

Sales managers should already understand the content, but they'll also need to know how reporting and analytics indicate gaps in the behaviors that were taught and how to coach to close those gaps. You can provide support materials to help them reinforce the training with reps, training on how to diagnose gaps, and how to coach as effectively as possible. You can also coach them on how to manage and lead their teams and excel at other aspects of their complex and challenging role. This is covered in more detail in the chapter on sales manager enablement.

Measures

We all know that what gets measured gets done, so don't leave this part out. Measurement addresses what success looks like and how you monitor results to determine if you're achieving the desired outcomes or need to pivot.

When measuring, you should:

- Include both leading indicators (the things that show progress toward a result) and lagging indicators (the end result)
- Measure what people have learned (such as progress reports, learning assessments, and feedback documentation)
- Measure post-training performance results (coaching sessions and metrics that indicate progress or results for whatever behaviors were trained)

Measurement plans are addressed in detail in building block 9: sales analytics and metrics.

Performance Management

According to the *State of Sales Training* reports published by ATD in 2016 and 2019, the top barrier to effective sales training is that salespeople are not held accountable for applying the skills learned in training. This metric was worse in the 2019 report (59 percent) than the 2016 one (50 percent), but both are the result of unclear expectations and poor performance management. It doesn't need to be this way.

Beyond the transfer plans and developmental coaching required to ensure training transfer and post-training success, every organization needs a great sales performance management system. Using what was taught in training (for reps) and coaching and developing reps based on that (for sales managers), should become part of the ongoing performance management in the organization. Both front-line sales managers and sales reps should be held accountable, and C-suite leaders should be asking sales leaders about it.

Change Management: An Integrated, Aligned Change Plan

Do you think change happens on its own? I believe you already know it doesn't work that way. People groan when I say that every sales performance improvement initiative is a change management project, but it's true.

If you've designed or chosen content that will improve results if used, it makes sense to create a plan for leading and managing the change necessary to get those results. It's a great start to:

- Get the various elements of the Sales Training System together.
- Get everyone aligned around those elements.
- Provide training and reinforcement for reps and managers.
- Continue tracking (measurement and reporting) and focus on getting the results you want.
- Overcommunicate about expectations, results, challenges, pivots, successes, and what's required to stay focused on the initiative until the change is cemented in the culture and becomes routine.

Whether you use John Kotter's eight-step change model, ProSci's ADKAR, McKinsey's 7-S framework, or another model, manage your key sales performance improvement initiatives like a change project—because they are.

THOUGHTS ON VIRTUAL LEARNING

In addition to the public health and economic impacts of the COVID-19 pandemic, the resulting lockdowns had a massive and immediate impact on the sales and talent development professions–namely, the immediate transition to virtual selling and virtual training. Almost overnight, all salespeople become inside sales reps, and all trainers and sales enablers became virtual trainers.

I've been saying for a while that the current technology would allow us to segue to virtual sales onboarding, virtual sales training, and even virtual sales kick-offs (SKOs), for anyone who cared to do so and had the design prowess to maximize the potential of virtual environments. (Or in the case of virtual SKOs, perhaps the budget for the proper virtual conference software.)

The remaining reasons to continue classroom instructor-led training or centralized events, most of which are social reasons, include:

- The confidence-inspiring visit to corporate HQ
- Unplanned water cooler interactions with executives or others
- Bonding with company leaders and onboarding cohorts during meals or other orchestrated social gatherings
- The costs associated with virtual training and conference platforms and the time and effort required to redesign programs to ensure they are effective
- Internal social pressure from those who don't understand how virtual events could possibly be as effective or just believe it won't work

Summary

This chapter shows how transformative systems can be. I described the first two of my four systems, the Sales Readiness System and the Sales Training System, and how their elements function collaboratively to support training and sales performance improvement. While the effectiveness of the sales readiness activity is determined by these elements and their execution, it's important to remember that every sales performance improvement initiative is basically a change management project. Prepare for change, guide the change, and cement the change. The last element in the chapter, performance management, leads us to coaching, and the building block for sales coaching.

7

Sales Coaching

Sales coaching is a substantial, vital subject and an essential building block that can have a significant positive impact on sales force performance. There are entire books written on sales coaching, so I am only going to hit the highlights of what I've seen make a real difference.

For a more in-depth exploration, I have developed a course on sales coaching excellence, which is available through SPARXiQ (see the appendix for a full list of recommended resources and references).

What Is Sales Coaching?

At a high level, sales coaching is a formal developmental process where sales managers partner with reps to improve performance. Sales managers encourage their reps to take responsibility for their growth by helping them determine areas of development, create action plans, and take steps to improve their performance. Instead of telling the reps what to do, sales managers act as guides to help them uncover the best strategies to achieve their goals, which creates a development partnership. To build the most effective sales coaching development programs, managers must know what, how, and why to coach. It might seem odd to some, but this building block also includes field training, which is what managers deliver, in contrast to training provided by a training department, HR, or sales enablement function.

If you want to develop a best-in-class sales force, your front-line sales managers need to:

- Analyze their sales reps' performance.
- Decide where to spend their limited coaching time to get the best results.
- Determine the best type of solution (such as training or coaching) and the right solution content:
    - Identify ways to help reps maximize performance in targeted areas.
    - Provide training to ensure reps have the skills they need to succeed.
    - Guide reps to greater success with a coaching approach that's engaging and motivating.
- Establish a regular coaching cadence to help reps attain sales mastery and achieve the best results possible.

In this chapter we'll discuss how you can make these things happen.

Using Metrics for Impact

The goal is to use sales analytics to help managers determine where to spend their coaching time to have the best impact on their team's performance.

When planning to work individually with a sales rep, most managers say something like, "Hey Ruth, I'm available to ride along with you on [date]. Where are you headed?" However, to make a more significant impact, the savviest managers will say something like, "Hey Ruth, based on our recent analysis, let's spend time together when you're working with prospects in [stage 2] moving toward [stage 3.] When can we schedule that?"

It's the metrics and analysis that managers do with their reps that allows them to target areas of development that will lead to the best-possible performance improvement.

There are multiple reports and dashboards that can support managers with this task. You probably have many in place already. I like to create a historical dashboard of the sales process stages, the number of opportunities per stage over the period reviewed (usually two to three times the average sales cycle), and the conversion ratios between stages. I group the sales force into anonymous buckets of top producers and average producers and compare their results to a specific manager's team (now named, rather than being anonymous), showing the team's average performance and the individual performance of each rep (Figure 7-1).

Figure 7-1. Rearview Mirror: Pipeline Analysis

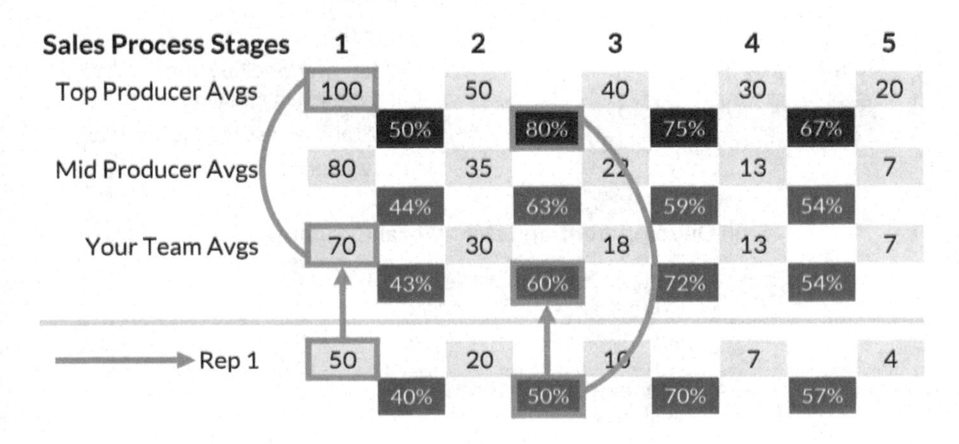

Opportunity Management: Sales Process Conversion
Sales Process Stages
1
2
3
4
5
Top Producer Avgs
100
50
40
30
20
50%
80%
75%
67%
Mid Producer Avgs
80
35
13
7
44%
63%
59%
54%
Your Team Avgs
70
30
18
13
7
43%
60%
72%
54%
Rep 1
50
20
7
4
40%
50%
70%
57%

As managers compare individual reps to their team averages and the other producers, they should be able to identify gaps quickly, which they can then explore more deeply using the methods outlined here. This report may require modifications based on context and nuance (that is, the unique business circumstances at your company), but you can figure that out with your leadership team and business analysts. Keep in mind that this is only one example, and doesn't apply if you manage business development reps or strategic account managers. It's the thought process that matters, and you can work to find ways to do this for all the roles on your team.

Activity and Methodology

Managers can use the ROAM model to analyze the targeted performance gaps and begin to hypothesize the root causes and possible solutions (Figure 7-2).

ROAM comprises these steps:

- **RO:** Compare results versus objectives (outcome gap) to determine where to focus. This is part of the review of sales metrics.
- **A:** Review or discuss the activities the rep is performing. This includes what they are doing, with whom, how often, and as applicable, when and where they're doing it.
- **M:** Review or discuss the sales methodology used for the buyer-facing activities. This is an examination of the quality or how well the activities are being performed.

Figure 7-2. How to Use ROAM to Analyze What to Coach

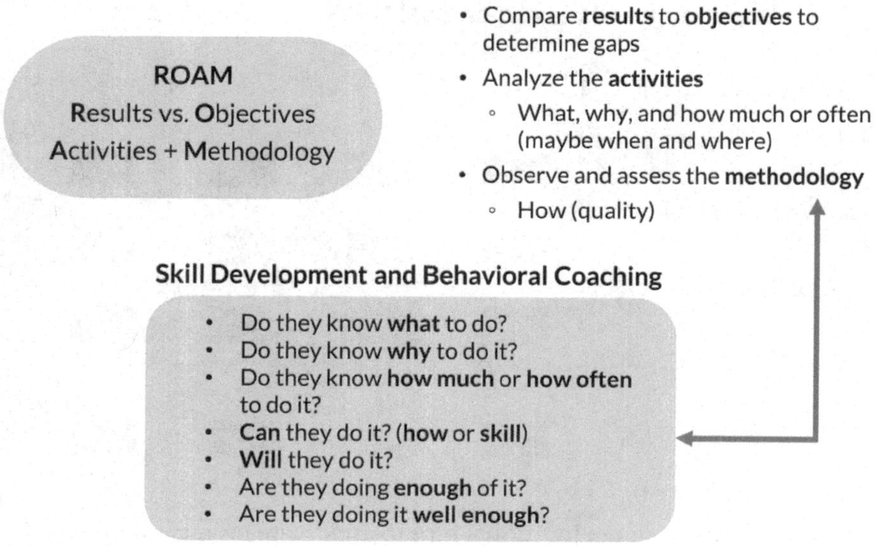

ROAM
Results vs. Objectives
Activities + Methodology

- Compare **results** to **objectives** to determine gaps
- Analyze the **activities**
    - What, why, and how much or often (maybe when and where)
- Observe and assess the **methodology**
    - How (quality)

Skill Development and Behavioral Coaching

- Do they know **what** to do?
- Do they know **why** to do it?
- Do they know **how much** or **how often** to do it?
- **Can** they do it? (**how** or **skill**)
- **Will** they do it?
- Are they doing **enough** of it?
- Are they doing it **well enough**?

From their previous knowledge of the rep's behavior and current discussions, managers should be able to formulate a hypothesis of the performance problem, which they can then explore further.

Root Causes

As managers explore the A and M of ROAM, they should go beyond discussion and their current knowledge of the rep's activities and the existing methodology used to observe their rep in action in targeted areas to acquire a fresh, new perspective. Observing the activities and sales methodology will help validate their hypotheses and identify the root-cause knowledge or skill gaps.

Solution Type and Content

Based on the reasons for nonperformance, managers can then determine the best solutions—the type of solution (training, coaching, or something else) and best-practice content that will close the gap.

Figure 7-3 contains the key questions we discussed earlier and shows where field training and sales coaching intersect.

Figure 7-3. Key Questions for Skill Development and Behavioral Coaching

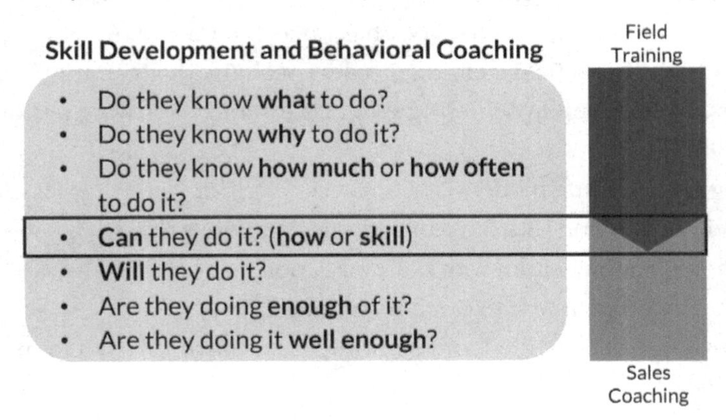

This works at the simplest level, but I have also adapted a conditions, reasons, and solutions for performance chart based on Ferdinand Fournies's book *Why Employees Don't Do What They're Supposed to Do and What to Do About It* to explain causes for non-performance, including reasons outside training and coaching (Figure 7-4).

Figure 7-4. The Conditions, Reasons, and Solutions for Performance

Condition	Reasons	Solutions
Don't Know Something	What to do	Train
	Why to do it	Coach
	How to do it	
Incorrect Thinking	Their way is better	Coach or Counsel
	Your way won't work	
	Something else is more important	Feedback
	They are doing it (lack of feedback)	
Misaligned Consequences	A negative consequence for doing it	Manage Consequences
	No negative consequence for not doing it	
	A positive consequence for not doing it	
	No positive consequence for doing it	
Constraints	Obstacles beyond their control	Counsel Change Transfer Terminate
	Personal limits (incapacity)	
	Fear (anticipating failure)	
	Personal problems	
	No one could do it	

Performance Analysis and Solution Design

The 16 reasons employees don't do what they're supposed to, and what to do about it.

Counseling, managing consequences, changing something within the organization, or transferring or terminating an employee are out of scope for field training and sales coaching, but are options you can consider, when appropriate. Engage your HR manager, as needed.

Field Training and Coaching

At this point, assuming the manager has uncovered a performance gap that can be addressed with field training or sales coaching, they can use these models to support their rep in achieving skill mastery and improving performance (Figure 7-5).

Using field training model:

- **Tell:** Instruction with a recap and understanding check
- **Show:** Demonstration with skills validation
- **Do:** Action plan with execution and tracking
- **Review:** Check ROAM and continue the train and coach loop, as needed

Using the sales coaching model:

- **Engage:** An engaging facilitated discussion about what and how to improve
- **Practice:** Role-play practice with debriefs and feedback loops
- **Do:** Action plan with execution and tracking
- **Review:** Check ROAM and continue the train and coach loop, as needed

Figure 7-5. ROAM

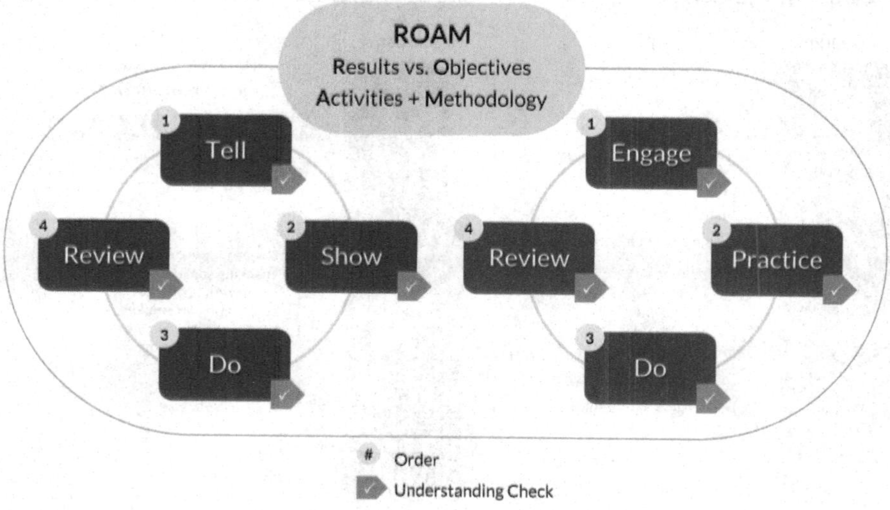

How to Conduct Field Training

You're ready for field training when you have:

- Conducted an analysis to know where you can have an impact

- Diagnosed the performance gaps by analyzing the activities and methodology compared to known best practices
- Determined what the rep needs to know how to do, why, and how it will close the gap by improving the activities and methodology

To do this, I offer the field training model with tell, show, do, and review (Figure 7-6), with the super-charger understanding check, which validates both communication and capability. This simple-but-powerful validation technique is significantly underutilized and critical to success.

Figure 7-6. Field Training Model (Tell, Show, Do, and Review)

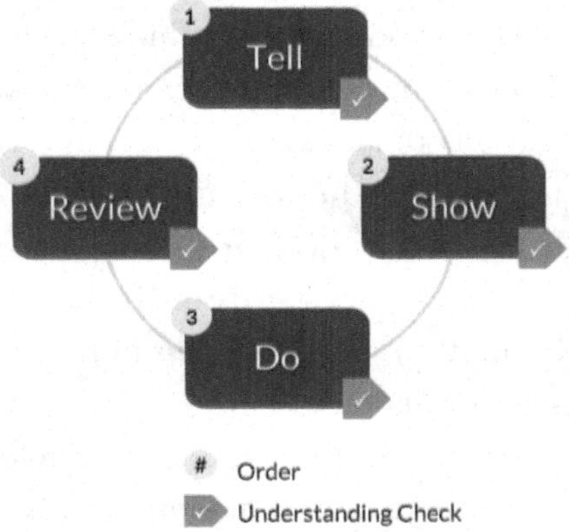

This mode is neither new nor complicated; it just works. The magic of this method, however, is in the disciplined execution of the four steps.

First, *tell* the rep what to do. Keep in mind that when you do this, you are training, not coaching. Being directive is acceptable for training so that reps are clear on what to do, why to do it, and how. It can also be highly effective to engage the rep to see what they already know, and then close any gaps. In the end, the most important outcome is that you've communicated and agreed on what you expect them to do. Then, use the understanding check to ask the rep to summarize what they think they are expected to do. Don't leave this stage until the rep can summarize it to your complete satisfaction.

Next, for skills-based learning, *show* them how it should be done, typically through role playing. Role play works best here because you can control the situation from a learning perspective. If necessary, you can also demonstrate live with a customer, have them role play with others who can demonstrate what should be done well, have them ride along with a top producer whom you know will demonstrate the targeted skill properly, or use a video demonstration, if you have one. For expediency and effectiveness, I recommend role playing in real-time with their manager. Then, in the understanding check, they role play the skill back to you. This validates that the rep not only understands it but can *do* it. It doesn't guarantee they *will* do it once they're on the job, but it does mean they *can*.

If you're not always able to do this step in person, you can use video and virtual coaching tools as well as live virtual role play services, or even web conferencing software using webcams, to support practice and feedback.

In the *do* stage, the manager or a seasoned rep should demonstrate the skills live—in a real selling situation—on the phone or in person. Some skip this step and move directly to live application with the sales rep, but I recommend first showing the rep how to use the skills effectively in a less clinical, real-world setting where unexpected things happen. In the understanding check for this stage, the manager observes the rep with a prospect or customer. This lets them assess whether the rep clearly understands expectations and validates that they *can* do it and *will* do it in live selling situations. It also allows managers to verify how well the reps can do it and coach them toward mastery.

If you can't get through these three stages successfully without a breakdown, it will never happen in the real world to any degree of certainty, regularity, or mastery.

Even if what's taught during field training is used by reps in the real world, it doesn't guarantee mastery. That's where the *review* stage comes in. After real-world observations, managers should meet with their reps to discuss and assess their performance together. This is still part of the overall training process because you are targeting a specific skill or set of skills that was just learned. This is where field training dovetails with coaching. You can also extend the review phase, as needed, with rolling review check-ins until the rep has mastered the specific skill you are teaching (Figure 7-7).

Figure 7-7. Rolling Reviews for Field Training

Who	Coach and Sales Rep
What	Phone call, virtual meeting, or face-to-face meeting
Why	Even the best players need a good coach to improve
How	• Review results versus objectives. • Review and discuss activities. • Discuss and observe methodology. • Continue to hone the targeted skill. • Reset performance goals, as needed. • Create an action plan. • Execute again. 4 Review

To recap, here's why the field training model of tell, show, do, and review is critical:

- It makes expectations clear for the rep and helps them develop the necessary skills to close their performance gaps.
- It is the ultimate excuse remover because you've seen your rep demonstrate that they understand what to do and know how to do it, which fosters accountability.
- Your upfront investment reduces the time spent on these skills in the future. My advice is to do it right once, rather than ineffectively and repeatedly.

If a rep doesn't use the skills they've been taught after a field training cycle of tell, show, do, and review or doesn't do them well, their manager can:

- Coach to help the rep improve on what they know.
- Begin to explore other reasons for nonperformance using the conditions, reasons, and solutions for performance chart, and addressing them as needed.

How to Conduct Sales Coaching

After deciding where to direct your coaching efforts and diagnosing performance issues with ROAM, you will train, coach, or apply another solution from the conditions, reasons, and solutions for performance chart.

You may determine that sales coaching is needed after you do field training with the tell, show, do, and review model with understanding checks (to continue toward mastery), or you may uncover an issue where going directly to coaching is the right solution. Other times, you will choose to coach the employee after training is complete (because they *can* do it, but they need to get *better*). Whenever skills coaching is the appropriate solution, you'll use the sales coaching model with engage, practice, do, and review with understanding checks (Figure 7-8).

Figure 7-8. Sales Coaching Model (Engage, Practice, Do, and Review)

In first step, *engage*, you'll involve the rep in a facilitated discussion about improvement possibilities. What do they need to improve, and how will you work together to accomplish that? If you're continuing from a previous training plan, your goal is already identified. If not, you'll need to start with (or may have just completed) a new diagnosis and plan.

This is different than field training, where you teach the rep what to do, why to do it, and how to do it. While rep engagement and involvement are important when training, this process should be far more facilitative, collaborative, and engaging. The manager should act as a guide, keeping their rep involved, thinking, problem solving, actively participating, and, ultimately, owning the solution—in this case, what to improve and how to do it.

As a coach, a manager should:

- Lead by asking questions to engage, foster involvement, and gain commitment.
- Draw out and remind the rep of best practices from onboarding, ongoing training, or previous experience and coaching sessions.
- Provide exposure to top producers or their call and meeting recordings, to introduce new ideas or best practices.

At the end of this step, your rep should have a clear path forward for improving the targeted skill and be able to summarize it for you with an understanding check.

In the second step of the model, *practice*, it's time to hone the decided-upon target skills and prepare to implement what you discussed and agreed on in engage. This is very similar to the show step in the field training model, except that now, rather than you demonstrating new skills to them first, your rep is practicing first with you to further hone their current or newly acquired skills. It's always acceptable to switch roles, if you think another demonstration might help, but this is your rep's practice time. As always, you should debrief with their thoughts first on what went well and what they'd like to continue to improve; then add your feedback or advice. (I recommended asking if you can provide feedback, at least for the first time.) Continue the practice, debrief, feedback loops until your rep can demonstrate an improved skill level to your satisfaction.

In the third step, *do*, it's time for your rep to document and execute their action plan. Give the rep room to try their plan, make mistakes, learn, and then change it. As they execute the plan, make sure they know they can reach out for support before you are scheduled to meet again. You can help them prepare for their first attempts by answering questions and offering advice as needed. Depending on the situation, you may want to observe or coach to assist in their action plan implementation. However, this is not a full-blown cycle back through diagnose, plan, do, and review; it's a way to provide support as they implement the plan. While this seems like a segue into the review stage, it's not. In this step, the understanding check occurs when the rep executes the plan as agreed, because the execution validates their understanding. But remember, this doesn't mean it will be flawless—this is developmental coaching, so you'll likely need to help them change their behavior incrementally before they reach mastery.

In *review*, the final step, you will meet with your rep for planned coaching, specifically to review the plan outcomes and results. In this session, listen to details, ask questions, gather information to understand what happened, assess how closely your rep's implementation was aligned to the plan, and see what results they achieved. Based on how the rep improved their skills and results, determine whether you need to cycle again through diagnose, plan, do, and review, or at least through ROAM, and whether you need to consider alternatives from the conditions, reasons, and solutions for performance chart. Then, verify communication with an understanding check to ensure mutual understanding about any additional plans or the path forward.

This is similar to extending the review stage for field training, but not exactly (Figure 7-9).

Figure 7-9. Extending the Review Phase With Rolling Reviews

Who	Coach and sales rep
What	Phone call, virtual meeting, or face-to-face meeting
Why	Even the best players need a good coach to improve
How	• Review results versus objectives • Review and discuss activities • Discuss and observe methodology • Continue to sharpen the targeted skill • Reset performance goals (as needed) • Create an action plan • Execute again

How to Conduct Individual Coaching Sessions

Throughout this chapter, we've focused on the process of diagnosing areas for improvement, determining solutions, and which models to use based on the circumstances. When coaches focus only on the process of sales coaching but lack the ability to facilitate, engage, and guide their reps, they may not produce the desired results. Great sales coaching requires both a logical process and great interpersonal skills.

If you are coaching, rather than delivering training, you should facilitate with questions and act as a guide (helping the rep figure things out, not telling or directing them unless absolutely necessary). The SLED model is effective for leading individual coaching sessions (Figure 7-10).

Figure 7-10. The SLED Model

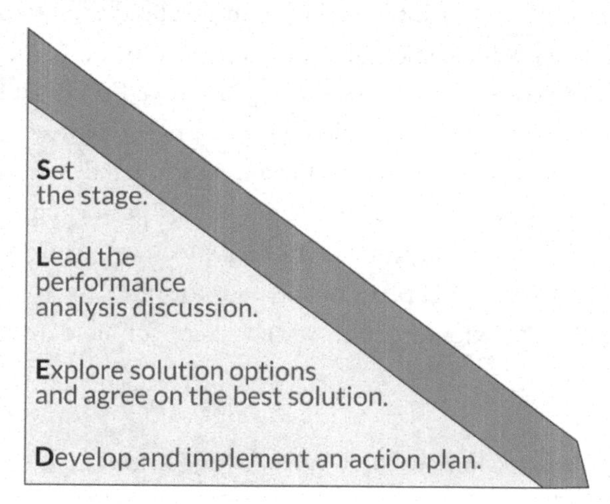
Set
the stage.
Lead the
performance
analysis discussion.
Explore solution options
and agree on the best solution.
Develop and implement an action plan.

Set the Stage

Start by discussing why you are spending time together so that it's clear to both parties. You do this by aligning on the purpose, plan, value, and timing for the session:

- Ensure roles are understood. The rep owns their development. You, as the coach, are the guide.
- Confirm that your intentions are understood—your aim should be to help and support your sales rep in achieving their goals and reaching their highest potential.

- Build trust. If this process is new for your rep, it may take some time to build trust in the approach.

Lead the Performance Analysis Discussion

In the second step, you'll:

- Discuss how you and the rep will prepare for the meeting and review any sales analytics together (sales metrics or sales competency diagnostics).
- Align on expectations and issues to be addressed (the competency gap to be closed, including the "what and why").

Explore Solutions and Options, and Agree on the Best Solution

In the third step, you'll:

- Schedule field observation or further diagnostics as needed to confirm any hypotheses you've reached together.
- When you have all the data you need or can obtain, consider solution options and select the best path forward. Remember to lead and facilitate, rather than direct. You can give suggestions if the rep gets stuck, but it should be a discussion.
- Deliver or schedule field training or sales coaching sessions, as needed, to support the skill development and performance improvement.

Develop and Implement an Action Plan

In this step, you'll want to include who will do what, how, and by when. In addition, you'll want to:

- Consider your employee's motivators to maximize the chance of the plan's success.
- Follow up and continue the loop through diagnose, plan, do, and review until the performance objective are achieved.
- Use SLED to run the individual coaching sessions.

How to Implement a Cadence of Coaching

From these detailed descriptions of sales analytics, ROAM, the coaching process, the outputs of field training or sales coaching with action plans, and the SLED model, you might assume that developmental coaching, as I've outlined here, takes a lot of ongoing time and effort.

It's true that learning any new skill and gaining mastery does require a front-loaded investment of time and effort. But I'm recommending coaching that can be easily integrated into a manager's day once they have the methodologies, skills, and tools like a pipeline analysis dashboard.

While well-orchestrated developmental coaching is critical for improving the performance of any sales team, there is nothing wrong with using coaching in-the-moment as an additional strategy. (Although it should not be the only coaching strategy you use.) To produce the best results, skill development and behavioral coaching should be consistent and purposeful. Establishing a Sales Management System with a Sales Management Operating System (a regular cadence of sales management activities and meetings) is one way to get into a rhythm where both types of coaching can occur.

Sales Management System

The Sales Management System will be detailed later in the book, but because of the tie to the coaching cadence and creating a coaching culture, I mention it here (Figure 7-11).

Figure 7-11. Sales Management System

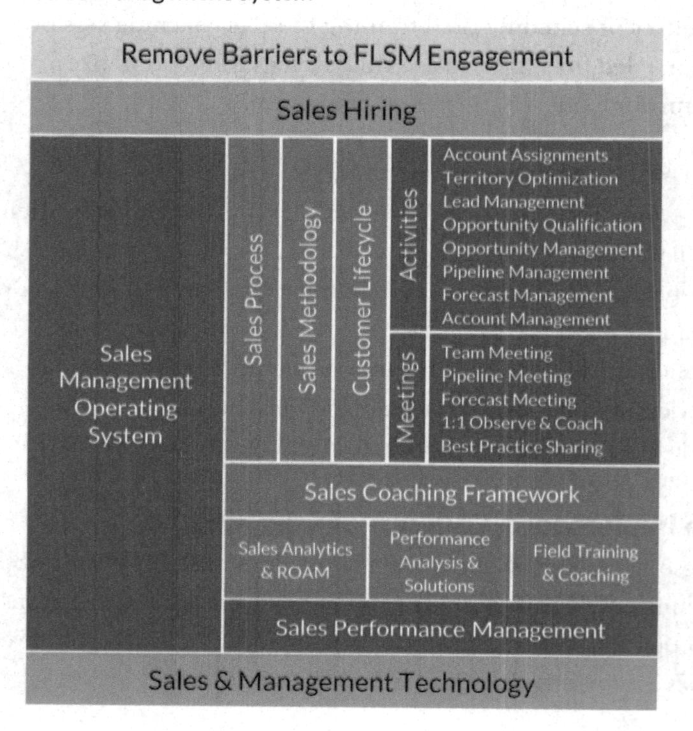

Getting into a cadence or a management rhythm brings many benefits. It creates a structure for how you run the business, fosters efficiency and effectiveness (especially for recurring meetings), provides consistency for employees and senior leadership alike, sets expectations for both you and your sales reps, and improves productivity. It also ensures that the most important things are receiving the attention they deserve.

From a developmental coaching perspective, establishing this cadence ensures that, despite the whirlwind of daily business, individual skills coaching won't be forgotten or ignored. The Sales Management System builds sales analytics, ROAM, performance analysis and solutions, and field training and sales coaching into the system.

By creating a coaching schedule, you'll have an opportunity to establish a culture of continuous improvement. In addition to team meetings, formal pipeline and forecast management meetings, and regular one-on-ones for problem solving and opportunity updates, managers should schedule monthly ride-along or call-along time with each rep. These are specific, developmental times where you can follow the practices outlined in this building block and help your reps grow and improve their skills in areas that truly matter.

Summary

To develop a best-in-class sales force, your front-line sales managers must be engaged because they are a force multiplier and a key performance lever. Managers support sales effectiveness by establishing a regular process of sales performance analysis and coaching, as described in this building block. The ROAM method helps you and your team identify performance gaps to maximize coaching efforts. The model offers a structure for disciplined execution. The diagnose, plan, do, and review sales coaching process in the framework can help you determine the best type of solution and the appropriate models to develop a coaching cadence, which is key to helping your reps attain sales mastery. Because it's part of creating a coaching process, I also introduced the Sales Management System. Now we're ready to take on our next building block—sales process.

8

Sales Process

Sometimes it seems as if the sales process is the most discussed concept in sales. Entire books have been written about it. It's frequently mentioned during discussions on LinkedIn. We toss the term around as if everyone understands it well and is managing and maximizing their sales process. However, this is not my experience.

We covered the buying process in chapters 2 and 3, but it's impossible to accurately explain sales process excellence without bringing the buying process into the discussion, so expect that and bear with me. That said, let's step back first and define a few things.

Sales process refers to the stages through which a sale progresses. Each stage has objectives, as well as tasks that are commonly performed to achieve those objectives. You need to complete exit criteria to move forward to the next stage. These concepts and terms are not unique to sales process. In fact, both entry and exit criteria are used in software development, Six Sigma, and some project management situations.

I could go deeper into additional process lexicon (entry criteria, milestones, and more), but I'm not sure it's needed. The understanding and purposeful management of these simple concepts is enough to manage the process effectively and improve sales results.

Not every task maps directly to an exit criterion and satisfies it. For example, a rep might need to set up a meeting with a new decision maker—that's a task. During that meeting, they might uncover, clarify, meet, and confirm acceptance of what they provided to meet that buyer's exit criteria for that stage. To think that setting up the meeting was an exit-criteria-related task, though, is a stretch. So, not all tasks are equal and not all will meet exit criteria.

Another thing to consider about tasks is the difference between logistical tasks and sales methodology. (Sales methodology is covered in building block 8.) Both are tasks, but sales methodology includes the buyer-facing, sales-related tasks and interactions, or how the reps sell (the frameworks, models, steps, and skills they use).

This is how the sales process (the stages, objectives, tasks, and exit criteria) and the special tasks (called sales methodology) fit together to create an excellent buying experience for decision makers and an empowering framework for sales reps.

Now, let's zoom out to look at the entire customer lifecycle, of which the sales process is a part (Table 8-1).

Table 8-1 represents one possible view of a customer lifecycle. In this case, I've aligned a sales process to the lifecycle, where alignment is possible. (When prospecting, you don't always know where your buyers are in the lifecycle before you contact them, which is why lead generation and management is a free-floating stage.)

As with the buying and sales processes, the lifecycle has stages, and each stage has objectives, tasks, and exit criteria. Here's how I group them:

- **Business planning:** This is the cycle of strategic planning or goal setting that most businesses go through. There is a wide variance of effectiveness and discipline around these activities, but most mature companies do some form of planning, goal setting, and budgeting activities.
    - For your sellers: If you approach buyers in this stage, they may or may not recognize the need for your support, unless it aligns with something they are already planning. Insight selling can be helpful in this stage. This is where you share relevant data, research, or your company's expertise and experience with similar customers to help your prospective buyers see around corners or avoid problems they are likely to experience. You'll have a better chance of creating interest if you can improve the likelihood of achieving their objectives (sometimes referred to as objective-based selling or outcome selling).

Table 8-1. Customer Lifecycle

		Business Planning			Business Plan Execution		Buying Process					Solution Execution		Status Quo
		Situation Analysis	Establish Strategy & Objectives	Create Tactical Plans	Implement Plans	Encounter & Assess Issues	Identify Possible Initiatives	Research & Compare Solutions	Compare Options & Select Solutions	Negotiate & Finalize Terms	Make Purchase	Implement Solution	Measure & Assess Outcomes	Run the Business
Customer Lifecycle	Objectives													
	Tasks													
	Exit Criteria													

Not intended to align withthe above customer changes

		Lead Generation & Management	Opportunity Management					Solution Execution		Lead Gen
Sales Process	Objectives									
	Tasks									
	Exit Criteria									
		Prospecting: Inbound and Outbound Research, referrals, omnichannel sequences, nurture,and monitor trigger events, and sales signals	Situation Assessment & Qualifying	Solution Development	Presentation & Proposal	Finalizing Details & Terms	Contracted & Closed	Deliver Solution	Measure & Assess Outcomes	Strategic Account Management

- **Business plan execution:** This is status quo for buyers, where they are executing their plans and going about their business. It's in this phase that things will either go very well or you will start to encounter issues with plan effectiveness or execution. When business leaders encounter problems, they often try to resolve them internally (do-it-yourself) and may succeed. However, if they struggle they may decide to seek external advice or assistance. (Or may they become open to a well-attuned seller who approaches them at this time—based on savvy research and problem-based prospecting—armed with relevant insights.)
    - For your sellers: If you approach buyers in the early stages of executing their plans, they may have a high degree of confidence in their initiatives and simply see you as an interruption or distraction. Insight selling or objective-based selling is also helpful in this stage. I normally recommend a problem-based prospecting approach (especially compared to a product-based approach), but this is the one place where it may not be as effective as it is elsewhere because the buyers may not yet be experiencing problems. This approach can work if you use insights or cases to predict issues buyers could encounter. Or you may need to focus on enabling the opportunities they believe they have and demonstrate how you can support their current plans and objectives to increase the likelihood of success.
- **Buying process:** This is the point where buyers begin to seek external advice and solutions to problems they think they can't solve on their own. Whatever their process, it ends with a decision to purchase, to do it themselves, or to remain with the status quo.
    - For your sellers: Problem-based selling is very effective in these stages. If you've been nurturing an account or buyers (account-based marketing or selling), or see a trigger event or sales signal in the alerts you track, this is an ideal time for an approach. Unfortunately, it may also be the most crowded time if your buyers are reaching out to other vendors, or worse, doing an RFP or already conducting a purchase pursuit with other vendors when you approach them. This is the best time for a consultative, buyer-centric, value-based, and outcome-oriented approach to differentiate yourself as much as possible from your competitors. And, as always, it's far better to create an opportunity than to

have to nudge your way in while surrounded by competitors or to scramble because you're late to the party.

- **Solution execution:** If the buyer purchases a product that requires implementation, this is stage in which the product or service is implemented and evaluated.
    - For your sellers: Depending on the price point of your solution, selling to replace your competitor's newly implemented product this stage can be incredibly difficult, unless your contact has massive buyer's remorse because of something that went horribly wrong very quickly with their current supplier. You may want to nurture this account to displace the competitor at some future point. If you handle yourself very well with the buyer and make a favorable impression (especially if the buyer expresses the wish that they'd connected with you sooner), it could be an opportunity for referrals to similar buyers they know in other companies.
- **Back to status quo:** After implementing a solution, the buyers return to the standard cycle of business planning and business plan execution (the status quo).
    - For your sellers: Factors that influence your ability to sell at this stage include how long ago your competitor's solution was purchased and implemented, the price point of your solution, your prospect's satisfaction with their current solution provider, or your competitive differentiation and added value. Considering variances in those factors, the best approach here might be the same as in either solution execution or business planning.

It's worth noting that the customer lifecycle diagram is not to scale or linear across any given company. These are important nuances to understand.

We all know that a company consists of departments and functions that are planning in support of the overall strategic plan and objectives, and executing projects relative to their function in the company. While your accounts are likely flowing through the lifecycle in a fairly linear way, multiple versions of this process are happening at the same time and are in various stages in each function. A prospect or account of yours, and the personas and functions you support with your products, may be in a buying cycle right now. At the same time, other personas and functions may be executing solutions they've purchased, while others are pursuing DIY solutions or are still in a planning stage.

So, in terms of sales process and enabling your sales force, what do you do with all of this information?

The most important thing is to map your sales process to the buying process and the rest of the customer lifecycle, where possible.

Once you've mapped your customer lifecycle and buying process (using expert market research and conversations with your customers and other buyers like them) and documented the generic market objectives, tasks, and exit criteria per stage, you can begin to align your process.

I often see people trying to align a prospecting stage to the buying process, but, in my opinion, this is a mistake. Of course, it's possible to know where a buyer is in their lifecycle (related to your company) when prospecting; reps can learn this through research, a referral, a common connection, or their personal knowledge of the company or people in it. And it's great when it works out that way.

However, sales reps often don't have access to that information and are flying blind until they speak to a buyer. That's why I set prospecting as a free-floating stage. When reps are prospecting blind, they need to determine where the buyer is through questions or listening to cues and clues from the buyer.

The rest of your sales process should be aligned to the buying and post-buying processes. Then, you should establish objectives, tasks, and exit criteria for those stages for your sales force. In addition to uncovering, clarifying, meeting, and confirming acceptance of your efforts to meet your buyer's exit criteria, sales reps have to complete their own tasks and exit criteria. For example, while reps should be buyer-centric, that doesn't preclude qualifying opportunities to ensure they are worth pursuing or have a reasonable chance of closing. Or, as another example, identifying and engaging with all decision makers in one stage might be a sales process exit criteria for progressing to the next stage. In this sense, building an effective, aligned sales process is very much like crafting an effective statement of work (SOW) or a mutual action plan (MAP). There are stages with objectives, tasks that both parties must complete, gated milestones, and timelines.

Considering the cross-functional collaboration aspect of sales enablement, you may not own the sales process design in your company. The sales operations team or even the senior sales leader may own sales process. In any case, you should understand the design work and collaborate to support the sales process, especially teaching how to maximize it, both during sales onboarding for new reps as well as with the current sales force.

Here are some other important considerations to keep in mind about the sales process:

- Desired outcomes and exit criteria may vary by buyer (each individual decision maker or influencer).
- Buying and sales processes may not be linear. Based on differences in exit criteria by buyer and how well sellers have met the varying criteria, different decision makers may be in different stages at different times. To manage the sales process most effectively, reps must pay attention to this.
- Reps should maintain forward momentum by building trust, demonstrating value, co-creating solutions with compelling outcomes, and messaging appropriately for various buyers based on what matters most to them and through meeting exit criteria. I also encourage reps to HAM/BAM, which is a fun acronym for "have a meeting, book a meeting"—meaning to book the next meeting during the current one.
- New entrants on the buyer side (decision makers or influencers), outcomes, or exit criteria will change things. Reps must be vigilant and adapt accordingly. This is why selling to multiple decision makers is described as the complex sale. It rarely becomes easy, but when reps better understand sales process, their own tasks and exit criteria in each stage, and how to manage their buyers' exit criteria, it does become easier.

Summary

"Sales process" refers to the stages through which a sale progresses; each stage has an objective with exit criteria that must be completed before moving forward. Think of an effective, aligned sales process as similar to a statement of work; there are stages with objectives, tasks to be completed, milestones, and timelines. It's important to remember that the sales process isn't the same as the sales methodology, which includes all the customer-facing selling tasks and their preparation. That is the subject of our next chapter.

9 Sales Methodology

Sales methodology includes the buyer-facing selling tasks and activities that reps do in each sales process stage and what they must do to prepare for them. This is not just *what* the reps do to sell, but *how* they do it.

More detailed than regular nonselling tasks (such as coordinating a meeting with multiple parties), the methodology includes the frameworks, models, skills, steps, and behaviors reps use (sales competencies), and how they perform those tasks—that is, how well (quality) they use those models and skills. This also includes the frameworks and models reps use to prepare to interact with buyers and execute the methodology.

Therefore, a sales methodology includes how to:

- Research and prepare for prospect buyers within a target account.
- Structure and execute that prospecting approach, using the research in a conversational framework.
- Open meetings effectively and run them well.
- Conduct discovery to uncover compelling problems you can solve or opportunities you can enable.
- Qualify an opportunity to gauge whether you have need and solution alignment (whether you can solve the problems or enable the opportunities you uncovered), whether you are talking to the right decision makers, and whether those buyers want to and can purchase a solution (and gauge the likelihood).
- Resolve buyer concerns in a buyer-centric way.

- Make effective presentations and personalize solution messaging by buyer (communicate value in relevant ways that will resonate with each buyer).
- Effectively conduct a quarterly business review (QBR) or what I call a customer value review with a current account.
- Properly set account objectives and develop account plans that will help you achieve them while more effectively serving your accounts.

Without naming names, many of the vendor sales methodologies we hear about most often are incomplete because they don't support the full customer life cycle. For example:

- Some vendors support top-of-funnel prospecting or outbound lead generation.
- Many vendors support how to conduct a sales call (although many are outdated for today's complex B2B enterprise selling environments and changing buyer behaviors).
- Perhaps an equal number of vendors include full opportunity management (although some ignore negotiating skills, which are critical).
- Some vendors only focus on a qualification framework.
- Far too few vendors support full strategic account management, key account management, or account management of any type.

The fact that a sales methodology is incomplete doesn't make it a bad methodology or a poor choice. It's just incomplete. The problem occurs when we say, "We use MEDDICC as our sales methodology," or "we're a Challenger shop; that's our methodology." I'm confident that both are excellent vendors who would tell you that their methodologies are impactful but not sufficient and do not address the entire customer lifecycle. It's when we think we're done with methodology work because we use SPIN that we fail our sales forces and ignore so many other things they could do to improve buyer interactions and sales effectiveness across the entire customer life cycle.

In addition to these "complete" (or not-so-complete) frameworks, there's a grab-bag of various other supporting skills, like time and task management and territory management, as well as newer methodologies, like insight selling and adaptive selling, that reps should be aware of and master.

Sales Effectiveness Acumens

There are other inputs—such as having the foundations of buyer acumen and business acumen—that will make your sales methodology more effective and allow real business conversations that help your buyers and differentiate you and your company. I call these foundational elements the Sales Effectiveness Acumens (Figure 9-1).

Figure 9-1. Sales Effectiveness Acumens

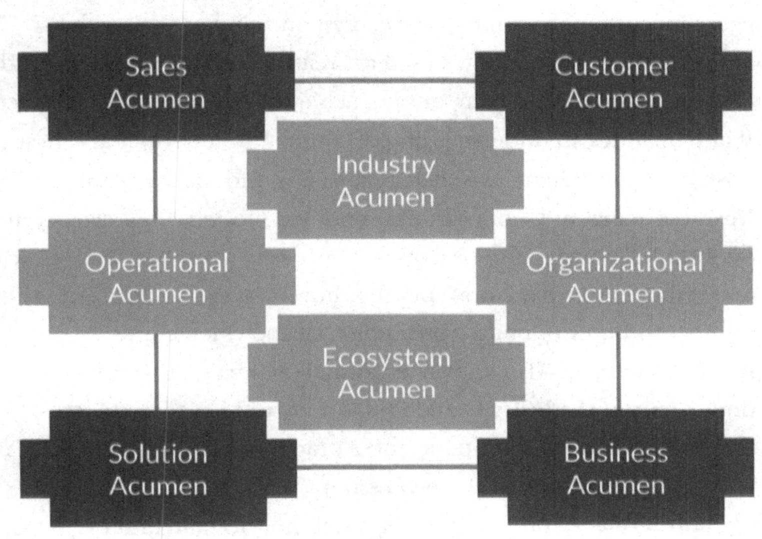

Let's look closer at each element:

- **Sales acumen:** Mastery in sales research, sales call planning, prospecting and lead generation, digital selling practices, opportunity qualification, consultative selling using an adaptive sales methodology (including discovery and situation assessment, solution development and co-creating solutions, developing proposals, conducting demos or presenting solutions and solution dialogue, resolving concerns, and gaining commitment), sales meeting management, multi-threading to message appropriately to buyers with different interests, storytelling, insight selling, negotiating, influence skills, consulting skills, general dialogue and communication skills, team selling, and strategic account management.
- **Customer acumen:** Understanding general buyer personas and buyer journey or buying processes, including COIN-OP (challenges, opportunities, impacts, needs, outcomes, priorities), decision process, decision criteria, decision roles, desired outcomes with metrics and

measures, and consideration of the decision makers' business and personal needs.

- **Solution acumen:** Understanding products and services and how they solve customer problems, critical thinking and problem solving, forcefield analysis, and how solutions tie to industry acumen, financial acumen, customer acumen, and ecosystem acumen. This is the culmination of acumens; it's used to create value for customers (and differentiation for the company) to achieve customers' desired outcomes. It also includes an understanding of competitive offerings and how to position against them, as well as against DIY and the status quo.
- **Business acumen:** Understanding business models, financial acumen, operational metrics and outcomes (such as key performance indicators and critical success factors), pricing, how customer organizations make money, and how to build a business case and calculate ROI.
- **Industry acumen:** Also known as domain expertise, this refers to understanding industry challenges, opportunities, technologies, regulations and legislation, business practices, current events and news, and the general state of the profession.
- **Organizational acumen:** Understanding how to plan and organize effectively; includes territory planning, account planning, sales call planning, leading sales meetings, task management, using CRM, sales enablement tools, other technology tools and performance support, action planning, calendaring, project management, change management, and personal productivity practices.
- **Operational acumen:** Understanding how to get things done and how to make things happen in your own organization and in others, including understanding processes, political savvy, culture fit, collaboration, consensus building, and the ability to execute on all the above plans effectively.
- **Ecosystem acumen:** Understanding vendor and channel partners and how to most effectively build relationships and engage with them to uncover, manage, and win opportunities through the effective co-creation of solutions for customers.

With these inputs and this solid foundation in place—and perhaps a healthy dose of interpersonal and communication skills—your sales methodology will be a lot stronger and your reps will be a lot more effective.

Whether you have the expertise internally to build your sales methodology or you decide to buy one (or several partial methodologies to sew together), you should consider conducting a top producer analysis. This is where you examine what your top producers do in comparison to other reps in your company and what industry best practices exist for each seller-buyer interaction that occurs along your customer lifecycle. Even if you don't use this analysis to build your own methodology, it will allow you to customize your purchased methodology for your organization. Conversation intelligence software—which records phone calls and sales meetings, allowing you to analyze them (sometimes with AI support)—is a great tool to enable your top producer analyses.

A word of caution here. There are software providers in this conversation intelligence category that publish their recommendations based on an analysis of their customer's aggregated recordings. There is potential value in this work, if done well, but I have real concerns about the research methodology used and some of the conclusions that a few of these companies draw from their "research," and I'm not alone in this opinion. I'd recommend extreme caution in accepting their recommendations as fact. Do your own research, preferably with the aid of an expert in data science and statistics.

The Fundamentals of Sales Effectiveness

The fundamentals of sales effectiveness operate like an assembly of separate cylinders positioned in outer and inner rings (Figure 9-2). First, you need a

Figure 9-2. Fundamentals of Sales Effectiveness

foundation of buyer-centric mindset and an understanding of how to create value from the buyer's perspective. These are pervasive across all other elements in the system. Then you master call planning, resolving concerns, and territory and account planning, which are required to yield effectiveness in the remaining life cycle and process-related elements. With these in place, you can follow the internal diagram to prospect, manage opportunities through your sales process, and manage the accounts you win.

Let's look closer at each element:

- **Buyer centric:** An outside-in mindset that considers everything you do from the buyer's perspective and influences your behavior to act in your buyer's best interest to achieve your success by supporting their success.
- **Value creation:** Your ability to understand what each buyer values and co-create solutions to deliver value and communicate the outcomes of your solution and the value you deliver. This includes business value (financial or operational metrics), experiential value (improving process or experience), aspirational value (aligning with mission, vision, and values), and personal value (meeting individual's professional or personal needs).
- **Prospecting:** The act of researching, planning, and approaching decision-maker contacts in target accounts to successfully generate interest in how you might help them achieve their goals, and setting an appointment to do so.
- **Discovery:** The act of understanding your buyer's situation and what matters most to the decision makers and key influencers—their current state and related impacts, their desired future state and related outcomes, and the size of the gap and the urgency to close it.
- **Opportunity qualification:** The act of analyzing various factors of the situation that typically indicate if there is an opportunity (a problem you can solve that is compelling enough to spur action) and whether the likelihood of winning the business is enough to commit the time, energy, resources, and money to pursue.
- **Opportunity management:** The act of purposefully uncovering and satisfying each buyer's decision criteria and buying process exit criteria to successfully shepherd the opportunity through the stages of the buying and sales process to a final win decision. Negotiating is included here.

- **Strategic account management:** The act of analyzing account potential, setting account objectives (after acquisition, it's usually grow, maintain, or recover but could also include retire), and considering relationships and other factors to build an account plan that will achieve the preset objectives, then executing that plan.
- **Territory management:** The act of analyzing the accounts and potential within your territory, however it is structured, to ensure proper account coverage and optimize the potential of the territory.
- **Account planning:** The act of setting account objectives and creating a plan to achieve them. Part of strategic account management.
- **Sales call planning:** The act of setting sales call objectives and then creating a plan to achieve them during the sales call or meeting.
- **Resolving concerns:** Buyers and customers may express various concerns at any stage of the buying process or customer life cycle. Resolving concerns is the act of following a buyer-centric process to acknowledge and clarify their issues to identify the types of concerns they have, so you can offer relevant perspectives and recommendations that address them effectively.

Determine What Good Looks Like

To be honest, even these fundamentals aren't complete when compared with the entire customer lifecycle.

There are a lot of tasks embedded in these fundamentals that aren't apparent in the figure and need to be teased out and documented, based on top producer practices or highly effective practices that are known to work. But it demonstrates the Pareto Principle, highlighting the 20 percent (in reality, possibly 40 percent) of things that top reps do very well to deliver 80 percent or more of their superior results.

It would be better if you had a recommended model that defined what good looks like, and a sales playbook that documented every *significant* seller-buyer interaction across that lifecycle. You should start with whatever is most important right now and prioritize based on your company's strategic plans for the year or an assessment of competency gaps. Eventually, you should work to cover the full lifecycle.

Then you should ensure that your methodology (every framework, model, step, and skill) is modern, buyer centric, consultative, value oriented, and outcome focused. It should also address the way modern buyers want to buy, based on the changes in purchasing behavior over the past years.

I'm not going to detail specific sales methodologies here, other than what I've mentioned already (which are not recommendations or endorsements), but make no mistake: Sales methodology is where the magic happens (or doesn't). I have developed several methodologies over the years for specific employers (based on a combination of known best practices and top producer analysis) and also implemented market-ready ones, which I customized for the business. Over time, I also have developed my own methodology to use as a starting point.

Speaking of which, I should clarify something that may seem confusing. I've been saying that many market-ready sales methodologies are not complete. I've also mentioned the Pareto Principle, relative to methodologies, which indicates that 20–40 percent of what top reps do produces most of their results. I recognize that might seem contradictory, but I don't believe it is.

What I'm saying is that you should purposefully ensure that you have a proven methodology and playbook in place across the entire customer lifecycle. Your methodology, however, doesn't need to be so complete or so detailed that no one can learn it, retain it, or use it. This is one reason that sales enablement leaders struggle to gain adoption of their chosen methodology, especially with some of the more substantial vendor methods. Some—even some that don't span the entire customer lifecycle—are so complicated or detailed that they are challenging to implement and gain widespread adoption or mastery. While I don't think it's a perfect 80–20 split, this is why I like conducting top producer analysis and applying the Pareto Principle to sales methodology. Finding the differentiating rep behaviors that make a real impact can help you keep your focus on what matters most.

The Fundamentals of Sales Effectiveness are a great place to start (or at least to guide your top producer analysis). If you get reps doing outstanding discovery and qualification, that alone will improve your sales results.

Figure 9-3 presents another example of focusing your methodology on the core things that will produce maximum results. This comes from SPARXiQ's Modern Sales Foundations methodology and course, which is a buyer-centric approach built from top-producer practices.

Lastly, there's a reason I recommend documenting the full lifecycle beyond the buying process. As I mentioned in the last chapter, when reps prospect they often do it the same way every time. This "selling by superstition" happens

Figure 9-3. A Buyer-Centric Selling Approach

Understand your buyers and decision makers:

- Roles & goals
- Challenges, opportunities, impacts, needs, outcomes & priorities
- Buying process with exit criteria
- Metrics that matter most

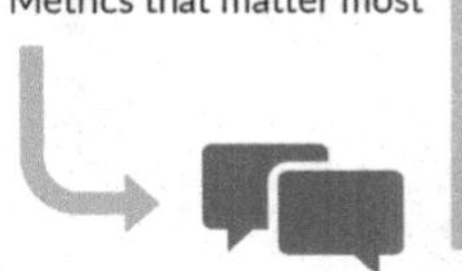

Flip the script to buyer-centric messaging:

- Focus on problems not products
- Discuss solutions to their problems
- Focus on resolving impacts and enabling outcomes
- Address both business and personal needs
- Tailor messaging by persona or person

Do exceptional discovery:

- Situation assessment
- Current state
- Future state
- Gap analysis
- Impact analysis
- Outcomes

Qualify the opportunity:

- Funding
- Alternatives
- Committee
- Timing and urgency

+

- Need and solution alignment

Co-create solutions:

- Build to solve problems
- Build to deliver outcomes
- Communicate value
- Message by persona or person

Manage the process:

- Uncover and meet exit criteria per stage
- Confirm acceptance of your support
- Gain commitments to move forward
- Keep your commitments and build trust
- Communicate regularly with clarity
- Manage both people and process

when reps do the same thing over and over with every buyer and hope for great results. If you understand the buyer's location in the lifecycle (through advance research or by uncovering it early in your initial interaction), you can adjust your sales approach. If you have strong buyer acumen, you can also adjust your approach and your messaging, personalizing as you go. For example:

- If the buyer is in a planning stage or early in plan execution, insight selling might work well to create an aha moment and help your buyers see the need for change.
- If your prospects are assessing issues or identifying possible solutions, normal problem-centric messaging with great discovery should work well.
- If your prospects are already comparing solutions, you'll need to find a way to differentiate yourself as a better solution to be considered in a purchase pursuit that's already in progress.

An advanced, adaptive approach to sales methodology that is truly buyer-centric will help your sales reps differentiate themselves and your company.

Summary

Your sales methodology is a wide-ranging collection of buyer-facing frameworks, models, skills, steps, and behaviors that span the entire customer lifecycle. While you want a proven, comprehensive method, it shouldn't be so complex that it can't be learned or retained by your reps. Consider the examples of how to create a buyer-centric methodology; the Fundamentals of Sales Effectiveness are a good starting point for guiding your top producer analysis and identifying impactful rep behaviors. This is foundational work before the next chapter on sales analytics and metrics.

10

Sales Analytics and Metrics

Having good analytics is a foundational element that underpins the Sales Readiness System and building block 9 of sales enablement. The metrics you track will enable the analyses you can perform. In that sense, this building block supports all the others and can help you gauge your effectiveness in each.

Whether it's data from your customer relationship management (CRM) software, learning management system (LMS), or sales content management (SCM; or sales asset management, SAM), applicant tracking system (ATS), sales performance management (SPM) software, or a separate business intelligence tool with drill-down dashboards, you'll want to determine the metrics that matter most for:

- Hiring effectiveness (time to hire, ramp-up times, new-hire production levels, turnover)
- Learning performance (progress, readiness metrics, and certifications)
- Content performance (what you have versus need and what's working best)
- Sales performance (during and after sales onboarding and ongoing sales force performance)
- Anything that you want to measure and improve

Understanding Lead and Lag Indicators

You may want to consider tracking lead and lag indicators for everything. Lag (or lagging) indicators are the outcomes or the end-result you want to achieve. Lead (or leading) indicators are the activities or interim results that forecast that you are progressing toward your desired end (lag) result. For example, the amount of exercise you do and the calories you consume over two weeks are lead indicators of whether your weight (the lag indicator) will increase or decrease.

Table 10-1 shows a few business examples in the categories of learning, content, and sales performance.

Table 10-1. Lead and Lag Indicator Examples

Lead Indicators	Lag Indicators
Learning Performance	
Courses started (on-time, late)	Courses completed
Assessments taken (on-time, late)	Assessment scores (pass/fail)
Pre-work completion	Assignment grades
Assignment completion	Role-play scoring
vILT attendance for ILT prep	Final validation or certification scores
Content Performance	
Number and percent of shares by asset, role and persona, process stage, and exit criteria	Correlation between asset usage and sales process momentum and conversion rates
Number and percent of buyer views, engagement, internal shares by asset or role, and persona, process stage, and exit criteria	Correlation between assets used and win-rates, loss-rates, deal size, sales cycle, and other sales outcome metrics
Number of rep shares by type of content and media	Buyer ratings of helpful and unhelpful content during a win-loss analyses
Number of buyer views, engagement, internal shares by type of content or media	Correlation of content used, buyer experience, and NPS, CLV, and retention stats
Sales Performance	
Calls, contacts, and campaigns	Wins and losses
Appointments set	Revenue and quota
Opportunities entered	Sales velocity
Presentations and proposals	Negotiated pricing and profitability
Sales process metrics (pre-decision conversion rates)	Sales process metrics (post-decision conversion analysis)

In a sales performance chart, the "appointments" set is listed as a lead indicator, but it can actually be lead or lag based on the role and circumstances. For a sales development rep who sets appointments for an account executive, this is a lag result. For an account executive who sets their own appointments and then manages those leads through the entire sales process, this is a lead indicator.

Also, the length of your sales cycle helps determine what to track. In most cases, both lead and lag indicators are helpful. But in the case of a very long sales cycle, such as 18 months, if you wait to track lag indicators, you'll miss the chance to identify possible problems early and intervene.

What Do You Need to Measure?

These charts are just examples, and while I could list every metric known to man, it's not possible to say exactly what's right for you in your specific business. You should consider each component of the Sales Readiness System to determine whether you have or want analytics for each, and if so, what they would be. Also, just because you can measure something, doesn't mean you should. Consider:

- What are you going to do with the results?
- How is it going to help you manage results, improve performance, or add value?

If it's not going to help you manage the business or improve business outcomes, you don't need to track it. The ones that you can use to manage the business, especially the lead indicators, make great dashboards.

Here are a few options that many don't consider:

- People don't often think of buyer personas or buying roles as something you would measure. However, you could track which were involved in each opportunity, which most often start deals, or which are most often your champion or financial buyer. If you know that, you can try to correlate it to conversion rates or win-rates. In one business, we learned that when a champion was involved, win-rates rose dramatically. (Note that this business clearly defined the parameters for what made a champion.)
- For sales methodology, there are many possible options, but you might want to incorporate a qualification scoring system in your CRM, which operationalizes your qualification methodology and takes buying process exit criteria into consideration (identifying and satisfying). This is also something you could correlate to win-rates.

- For overall sales methodology, you could use a competency assessment or skills certification program and correlate to ramp-up times or quota attainment.
- Business acumen could also be measured with an assessment or simulation score and correlated similarly.

You get the idea. Consider each component of the system and do what makes sense, adds value, can be tracked, and can be turned actionable in some way, whenever possible.

Keep in mind that there is a difference between business management metrics and performance diagnostic metrics:

- Business management metrics are what you want to track to show progress toward a goal or that give you a quick view of the current state or coming-soon state of your business.
- Doing performance diagnostic work to find root cause problems or how to improve performance often requires a more in-depth look.

To do both, you must track more than surface-level metrics, so they are there when you need to drill down. This does conflict a bit with my advice to not measure things just because you can, so it requires some experimentation. When I enter a business as an employee or consultant or start a new sales enablement department, I tend to establish a lot of measurement upfront to assess the current state, and then pare back over time once I know what's not needed in the long term. And, if it's easy and automated, I'll let the tracking continue without reporting it, just in case it's needed later.

There are many sales outcome metrics and sales process metrics. Let's take a deeper look. There's TOFU, or top of funnel management (outbound) (Figure 10-1).

The example in Figure 10-1 is for outbound phone prospecting, but it could be modified to include any type of outreach. Today, TOFU also includes demand generation and inbound lead management from marketing.

Then there is MOFU and BOFU (middle and bottom of the funnel management), or just opportunity management (Figure 10-2).

In all cases, you can measure lead indicators (activities) and lag indicators (results), both in raw numbers and conversion ratios between tasks and activities or stages.

By benchmarking points in time, you can measure the impact of your hiring practices, training programs, content releases, or other initiatives by comparing

Figure 10-1. Top of Funnel Management

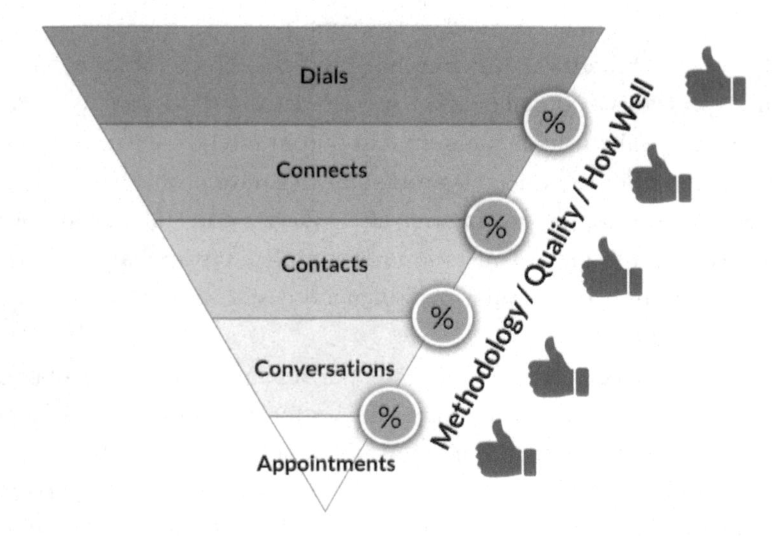

Figure 10-2. Opportunity Management

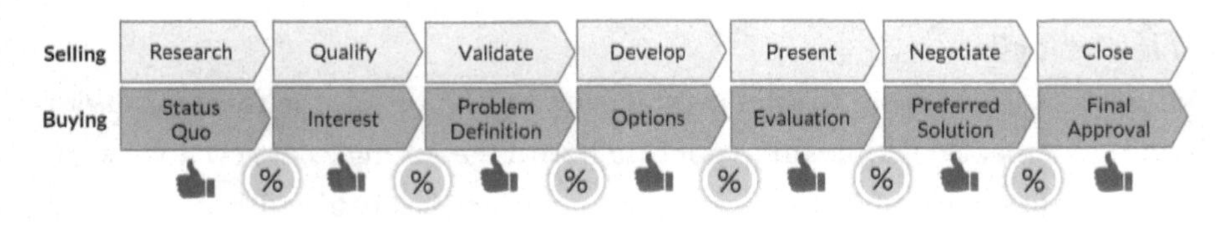

new results to old benchmarks (accounting for seasonality and other factors, of course). If this isn't a strength for you, you can involve a business analyst, data scientist, sales operations pro, or a consultant to establish sound practices while you are learning.

In addition to the metrics related to demand generation, pipeline management, and so on, you should consider tracking other things as they pertain to your business. Some potential metrics include:

- Average sales price
- Average sales cycle (including time in stage)
- Cross-sell and upsell
- Ramp-up times for sales onboarding
- Quota attainment (and YTD tracking toward it)
- Sales productivity
- Sales velocity

Let's take a closer look at sales productivity and sales velocity.

Sales Productivity

Sales productivity is often defined as "revenue per rep"; however, I prefer to describe it more broadly as "the output of the sales force over a given time." You can express this as a total or as an average per rep (both can be helpful).

While many sales leaders measure that output solely in terms of revenue, I like to consider both revenue and profitability. (You've probably heard the old joke, "How do we lose money quarter after quarter and still stay in business? Volume, volume, volume!") Unless you're running a startup that needs to show customer acquisition and revenue growth at any cost to secure funding, it's *profitable* growth that matters.

Simply stated: Total revenue, revenue per rep, and profit percentage for a given period, compared with the same metrics for a previous period (previous quarter, for example), gives you a quick, high-level view into whether the sales force is doing better or worse. That's sales productivity. Some sales experts will say that productivity is the time spent selling. That's a logical element of productivity but it's very difficult to measure. I find that output is a far more reliable metric.

Sales Velocity

Sales velocity is a cousin to sales productivity and is possibly the most misunderstood sales metric. People often confuse it with the average sales cycle. Instead, it's the "miles per hour" of your sales force, or how fast you're driving revenue. It's useful for forecasting but is an even better diagnostic tool.

To determine sales velocity, pick a period, such as the past year or quarter, and gather:

- Number of opportunities pursued
- Average sales price
- Average win-rate
- Average sales cycle

Then, run this formula:

$$\text{Number of Qualified Opportunities} \times \text{Average Sales Price} \times \text{Win-Rate Percent} \div \text{Average Sales Cycle} = \text{Sales Velocity}$$

You can use this formula to calculate sales velocity for your entire sales force, a region, a manager's team, or an individual. Based on the context, you might need to do it by product line as well or segment it in other ways. Feel free to experiment with segments, as well as the types of averages you use (that is, mean, median, and mode).

The one caution I'd offer about calculating sales velocity this way is the use of averages. Averages can be problematic in a variety of ways, so they should be worked with purposefully and cautiously. Occasionally, I'll remove outliers; experiment with mean, median, and mode; or convert to raw numbers for individuals or teams. You can calculate sales velocity over any period for an individual product, the whole company, or a single region, division, team, or individual. This flexibility is valuable in making comparisons. I recommend using sales velocity to:

- Look for indicators that improvement is needed.
- Determine where to probe more deeply.

If you compare a select group of top producers with others, it can help you identify where to explore further or coach to improve a team's performance or "move the middle" of your sales force. You can change the period examined so that it's relevant for your organization and measure velocity in days, weeks, months, or quarters, based on your sales cycle.

For clarity, you can get to the same place (the speed at which your sales force produces revenue) with "revenue divided by time," but that formula does not give you as many variables to explore to improve your outcome. With the earlier formula, you can further drill down into the opportunity number, deal size, win rates, and sales cycle to find opportunities to improve velocity. Some tips:

- Use qualified opportunities (versus suspect deals) and the win rate for those well-qualified opportunities. Unqualified opportunities are noise in the signal.
- You can express the sales cycle average in days, weeks, or months to get the time perspective that's right for your business.

As you experiment with velocity and work to improve the various metrics used to calculate it, just remember that profitable revenue is ultimately what matters most, so don't lose focus on other profitability measures.

Measuring the various elements of your sales enablement efforts and their impact on the sales force is an essential part of any sales enablement leader's role. While you may need the support of an expert for a while, I hope this chapter has given you some valuable things to think about.

Summary

The sales analytics and metrics in this building block are the foundation of the Sales Readiness System. The metrics you track enable the analyses you can perform. So, this building block supports all the others and helps you gauge your effectiveness in each. Once you understand lead and lag indicators, you should consider what you need to measure, asking yourself what you're going to do with the results and how you're going to add value. The tools and technology that can assist your analyses are discussed in the next chapter.

11 Sales Technology and Tools

In my sales career, I've worked for a leading sales enablement and readiness solution provider, I've worked closely with another through a client, I partner with a third provider at SPARXiQ, and I have been a strategic product advisor for several others. I've had hands-on trials or experience with a dozen others and have learned about even more through trade shows; sales analyst reports; software review sites; Nancy Nardin's company, Smart Selling Tools; and Dan and Megan Cilley's company, Vendor Neutral. Even so, I don't claim to be an expert in all the sales technology tools, or to even know them all. (Software tools are like the P.T. Barnum quote about suckers—there's one born every minute.) Despite the growing number of tools on the market, I do have a decent working knowledge of them and a strong understanding of the software categories that analysts review. Some (but perhaps not all) of those categories include:

- CRM
- Business research
- Buyer intent software
- Trigger event tracking and alert management
- Sales intelligence and business intelligence
- Account targeting
- Contact sourcing

- Sales engagement, prospecting, and lead management
- Video selling
- Guided selling
- Sales readiness
- Conversation intelligence
- Sales content management and sales asset management
- Scheduling and calendaring
- Presentation management
- CPQ (configure, price, quote)
- Proposal management and document management
- Workflow performance support (playbooks and guided selling)
- Contract and e-signing
- Sales coaching
- Sales compensation
- Sales performance management (SPM)

If you're not dizzy, I applaud you—it's hard to keep up.

The right tools, when implemented well, can increase both efficiency and sales effectiveness. The challenge is that there are so many and they all seem to make wild claims about their impact. Tool budgets vary based on company size, but ongoing research indicates that, on average, companies spend between $100 and $1,000 per sales rep per month on their sales stack. I've heard anecdotally that some well-funded SaaS startups invest multiple thousands of dollars monthly per rep, but I don't have hard data to back that up. Little surprises me anymore.

My most important advice on technology tools is twofold: buyer beware, and fix process and workflow first (or at a minimum, figure out exactly what you are trying to optimize and what it will get you). It's so easy to be seduced and distracted by cool tools, the latest features, and, lately, the power and potential of artificial intelligence and machine learning. Be clear about what you're trying to accomplish and support, in advance, and seek purposeful solutions rather than spending time with every tool vendor who calls, listening to pitches and watching demos for disparate, disconnected solutions. Since stringing tools together can end up somewhere between Frankenstein's monster (often called, with a grin, a "Frankenstack") and a patchwork quilt, I lean toward integrations and vendors who solve multiple problems (whenever possible) versus a series of point solutions. You need to figure out what's right for you, but whatever that is, be purposeful. There are limits to budget, sales force mindshare and attention, and the ability to implement and gain adoption. I tend to focus on tools that:

- Help support a system, such as the Sales Readiness System or the embedded Sales Training System.
- Help manage, share, and track content usage as an enabler for buyer engagement (with content that supports their exit or decision criteria). It works best if the collateral can be served up to reps in the context of the buying or sales process in their workflow (CRM).
- Help with research, lead generation, and prospecting.
- Serve up training content, reminders, other performance support (forms, job aids, worksheets, cheat sheets), insights to use, or playbooks, when the reps need them.
- Provide real-time workflow support for the adoption of best practices for lead generation (such as sales engagement platforms or SEPs, opportunity management, and strategic account management).

How Software Tools Support the 5 Stages of Sales Mastery & Behavior Change

Let's look at an example of how tools can support a process or something you're trying to accomplish with your sales force. When I first started sharing the information in Figure 11-1, it took between five and six different software products to support all aspects of the five stages of mastery. Today, while I could still string together point solutions, I could also do it with one.

Figure 11-1. How Software Tools Can Support the Five Stages of Sales Mastery

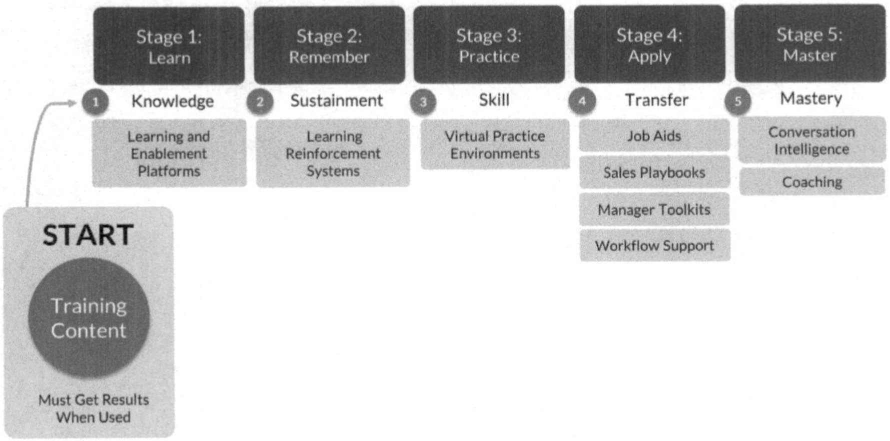

If I were looking to select or update my sales or sales enablement stack today, I would look to two resources: Nancy Nardin of Smart Selling Tools and Dan and Meghan Cilley of Vendor Neutral. They can provide more guidance and support than I possibly can in a book chapter.

Summary

The right tools, if used properly, can increase both efficiency and sales effectiveness. (Remember to aim for effectiveness first.) The challenge is choosing the right tool from so many, and resisting wild claims about their potential impact. To choose your tool wisely, ensure that you're selecting to support a process and workflow that you've established. Refer to Figure 11-1 with the 5 Stages of Sales Mastery & Behavior Change—which I introduced in the Sales Training System and that supports the sales training building block—as an example to see how a prospective tool (or tools) may support your organization across your sales motions.

12 Sales Compensation

I don't consider myself a sales compensation expert. I'm not embarrassed by that fact, and I obviously don't hide it. Personally, I think that sales compensation is largely broken and needs a massive overhaul. (Of course, I say the same thing about the sales profession in general, so maybe I just like to overhaul things.)

All that said, my lack of deep expertise here highlights my point about the power of and need for cross-functional collaboration. I have survived and thrived in corporate sales performance improvement leadership roles and as a sales consultant, delivering great results, without being an expert in sales compensation. I know there are others who disagree with me, but I've found that sales comp changes drive less organizational performance improvement than the other systems I've developed. (However, I do want to be clear that I'm not saying sales compensation is unimportant or that it does not influence performance. I'm saying that in my experience, its impact simply isn't as significant as the other systems.)

If you attended business school or enjoy reading management theory, you might remember learning the two-factor theory, which is also known as psychologist Frederick Herzberg's motivation-hygiene theory. Herzberg's theory states that there are factors in the workplace that cause job satisfaction, while the lack of other factors cause dissatisfaction. He defined these as motivation and hygiene factors, respectively. The hygiene factors include things like salary, fringe benefits, paid insurance, investment plans, and vacations. What's interesting is that his research indicated that these factors, including compensation, do not lead to positive satisfaction or higher motivation. However, dissatisfaction results from their absence or if they are viewed as less than desirable.

So, according to Herzberg, the absence of a comp plan that is deemed desirable and fair will lead to dissatisfaction. However, the presence of a desirable and fair plan will not necessarily motivate someone in the long term. It's for this reason that I've always thought of sales compensation as necessary, but insufficient. You may not always gain a lot from it, but it will certainly hurt you if you mess it up.

MOTIVATION AND MONEY

Herzberg's theory has advocates and detractors, and there has been much subsequent research on motivation and work satisfaction. If you want to dig in, the research is out there, and you can find a surprisingly good overview on the Wikipedia page for two-factor theory.

You've likely heard someone say sales professionals are "coin-operated," meaning they are highly motivated by money. This may be true to a degree, or perhaps to a greater degree than in other professions, but the motivation that truly fuels behavior is often intrinsic, coming from inside the individual. As Dan Pink posits in his book *Drive*, purpose, autonomy, and the desire for mastery are factors that fuel intrinsic motivation. This is why creating the right environment and culture to support high performance is so critical. Yet, compensation still plays an important role, because others are motivated extrinsically, or by outside factors (like rewards, incentives, and recognition). My purpose for laying this groundwork is to share that getting it wrong may hurt you more than getting it right will help you, and getting it right will help you more with some than with others.

Allow me to share a story of my first real involvement designing a sales compensation plan.

In the early 1990s, I worked in the headquarters of a Fortune 25 financial services firm, leading their national sales training team. I sold for this company and ran a branch sales office before becoming a sales trainer, training manager, and eventually their national sales training manager. My history in the field and the success of our training programs earned me a seat at the table with the leadership team. For that reason, I got to be involved in a series of projects, such as improving our sales hiring, sales manager development, and, one year, tackling our sales compensation issues.

We all knew we weren't getting comp right. For three years straight, maybe four, management changed the plan annually. The field was annoyed, believing that the carrot kept moving; the company wasn't getting the exact results they wanted either.

You know what was interesting, though? In hindsight, each year, as you examined the plan and what it was designed to compensate, you could understand why it drove the behaviors and results it did. One year, the plan emphasized volume (revenue growth). And so the sales force delivered growth, even if they had to discount so much to do it that it wasn't very profitable growth.

After a few years of missing the mark, the senior leadership team formed a committee to address the sales compensation issues and hired a very reputable consulting firm with specific expertise in designing sales compensation programs. The committee's role was to ensure all the issues of the past were examined, and that all perspectives were represented and understood by the consultants. The consultants' role was to ensure the committee produced a long-term plan that would deliver the results the company wanted, without inciting a riot within the sales force.

As with strategic planning, we started with the end in mind and worked backward. In a very collaborative, cross-functional environment, we considered these things:

- What were the plans of the past and what results did we get? Do we understand why?
- What is the budget we have to work with?
- What outcomes do we want, going forward?
- What behaviors will deliver those outcomes?
- What else do we want to reward?
- If you reward these things (outcomes, behaviors, and so on), will our plan drive the right behaviors and outcomes from our sellers?
- Do we have the capability to track the measures required and calculate the plan payouts?
- What will the payouts be at each level of performance, and does that fit within the budget of what the business can pay, while meeting profit targets? (That is, modeling.)
- Is the plan flexible enough to be modified annually based on changing factors, without a complete redo?

- Will our sales force understand the plan and be able to make selling, pricing, and negotiation decisions wisely based on it? (Or, as I heard someone say recently, "Can they calculate it themselves on a napkin with only a smartphone calculator?"
- When sellers "figure out the plan," what unexpected or unwanted behaviors might it drive?
- How does our plan compare in our market (the on-target earnings or total sales compensation for each role, compared to our competition)?
- Does it need to be tailored by role, and if so, can it be?
- How will you track and report plan progress, calculations, and payouts?

Then, guided by the consultants, we learned about the various compensation elements we needed to understand and what factors we should consider:

- **OTE (on-target-earnings):** This is the total compensation expected when reasonable targets and quotas have been reached.
- **Pay mix:** This is the plan components and weightings for each, including things like base, bonus, commissions, draw, MBOs (management by objectives or goals and tasks to be completed). A common mix is 60 percent base and 40 percent bonus or commission.
- **Add-ons and modifiers:** These includes spiffs or motivations, such as a bonus dollar amount for every new logo (to prioritize account acquisition).
- **Minimum qualifiers:** This might be a level the rep must achieve before they will be paid incentive compensation. Companies may elect to not pay commission on deals with discounts over 40 percent or a gross margin below a certain percentage. Or they may not pay out an annual bonus if reps achieve less than 70 percent of their annual quota. (See also *decelerators*.)
- **Accelerators:** These incent a higher level of performance by increasing payouts after achieving a predetermined level of performance. For example, they could include increasing the commission percentage by 0.5 percent for every sale with a profit margin of over 25 percent. Another might be paying a higher commission percentage after a monthly, quarterly, or annual quota is achieved.
- **Decelerators:** Similar to minimum qualifiers, decelerators are takeaways—they penalize underperforming reps and pay less or not at all, based on low levels of performance.

Figure 12-1. The Sales Comp Plan That Worked

Total Payout Buckets (Annual Amout): Bonus $20k; Margin $30k; % YTD Plan $50k

Base

Paid Biweekly

- Base salary of $x annually
- $x ÷ 26

+ Commission

Paid Monthly

- 1.5% of revenue per sale, on deals with margins of 12.5% minimum
- Capped at $25,000 per sale

+ Bonus ($20k)

Paid Quarterly

- Paid on revenue of:
  - X+: $5,000
  - A-B: $2,500
  - C-D: $1,500
  - < E: $0
- Deals below 12.5% margin do not qualify
- Target dollars in bucket are forfeited if revenue goals are not met

+ Margin ($30k)

Paid Quarterly

- Margin goal: 15%
- Paid per quarter
  - No payout at <15%
  - $5,000 at 15–18%
  - Up to an additional $2,000 at 18.01–20%
- Target dollars in bucket are forfeited if margin goals are not met

+ % YTD Plan ($50k)

Paid Quarterly

- Paid per quarter on a sliding scale:
  - <85% of plan = $0
  - 85.01–98.9% of plan = same % x $10,000
  - 99–105% of plan = same % x $10,000
  - 105.01–125% of plan = same % x $10,000
- Not forfeited quarterly
- Back bonuses can be earned if caught up to plan YTD in a subsequent quarter

- **Draws:** There are a variety of draw options. A draw is money paid to a rep in advance of commission earned. Sometimes this is done for new hires. Some draws are not recoverable. Others are recoverable, which means commissions are reduced or not paid until the draw is recovered.
- **Clawbacks (customer churn):** These are designed to recap commissions paid, often for an ongoing subscription service, when the customer cancels within a predetermined time period (such as the first 90 days).
- **Unlimited versus capped:** This is very simple. Some plans are built with no limits. Land a monster deal or crush your quota by 250 percent and get paid a monster commission or 250 percent of your target. Other plans limit the payout in some way, such as a maximum commission for one opportunity of $25,000.
- **Payout frequency:** During my 35 years in the profession, I've seen everything from daily cash payouts for 100 percent commission plans to weekly, biweekly, quarterly, biannual, and annual payouts.

So what happened in my story?

Glad you asked.

We created a comp plan that was unlike any of us had seen. I can't remember it exactly—it was almost 30 years ago. However, I do remember the concepts, and it looked something like Figure 12-1.

The plan was a structure that allowed for multiple earnings categories that could be adjusted annually, based on what was important to the business that year. For example, you could emphasize or de-emphasize revenue, margin, percentage to plan, discount percentages, product lines, cross-sell percentages, or whatever was key for the year.

My example in Figure 12-1 is an "all plusses" example, meaning it's additive across the board, with no major take-away elements. But you'll notice in commissions and quarterly bonuses, any deals below a 12.5 percent margin do not qualify.

Some of the categories have a predetermined maximum amount that can be earned, which are in the buckets at the top. In at least one bucket (percent to plan YTD), to earn it all the rep must overachieve, not just hit 100 percent of plan. In this category, the funds do not expire from quarter to quarter but can be re-earned by catching up to plan. In the other categories, the available funds for that quarter expire by quarter.

This was not exactly a back of the napkin calculation, but the sales force loved the plan. It took little time to figure out how to maximize it for the year, and the company adjusted reporting to ensure reps had what they needed to make good selling, pricing, discounting, and negotiating decisions to deliver what the company wanted and maximize their earnings.

I left this company a few years later. Interestingly I heard from a friend when the company was acquired many years later and US operations were shuttered, that our plan was still in place. I'd love to take credit for that, and while those of us on the committee had a lot of input, the consulting company gets the bulk of the recognition for that one.

I learned quickly as a new employee at a different company that the comp plan was a source of contention for the field. So I engaged HR and compensation leaders, who were also new (we were building a performance team), and collaborated with them to help them understand the challenges from the field perspective and the errant behaviors the current plan was driving. After that, I was able to get out of their way for the most part because I was more focused on building a new enablement function and addressing hiring, training, and sales management issues.

In another company, to support the success of a new sales onboarding program, we used incentive MBOs (management by objectives or bonuses for goal achievement) for both sales reps and their managers when new hires achieved performance milestones in a certain timeframe. This incented the new reps and their managers to take the onboarding lessons and activities seriously, as well as the related reinforcement and coaching, and rewarded success appropriately.

Like my experience, your level of involvement in sales compensation may be varied. Or, as some enablement professionals have been telling me lately, you may have compensation under your umbrella. I tend to think that many of us will continue to collaborate with HR and compensation pros and external experts for the design of compensation systems.

Since this topic is quite extensive and requires specific expertise, I included some recommend books on the topic in the resources section that you can review for a deeper dive.

Summary

The importance of an effective sales compensation plan and other strategic incentives can't be understated. However, they can also be a source of contention and drive unexpected behaviors to meet targets. Consequently, getting your plan wrong may sometimes hurt you more than getting it right. While your level of involvement in setting your sales compensation plan and incentive plans will vary, be aware of the range of compensation elements for your sales force and what you can do to maximize their impact.

13 Sales Manager Enablement

We all know that leadership development has been around for many years. The concept of sales manager enablement, however, is still emerging. While most standard leadership development applies to front-line sales managers, it isn't sufficient; sales managers have special requirements.

So, for the building block on sales manager enablement, I'll focus specifically on the specialized needs of sales managers while acknowledging that they should also receive standard managerial and leadership development. Sales managers especially need a solid foundation in setting expectations, goal setting, active listening and communication skills, leading meetings effectively, and the skills required to implement sales performance management, which is part of the system that supports this building block. That system is the Sales Management System (Figure 13-1).

The Sales Management System

Note the larger number of components and the complexity of this system when compared to the others we've discussed. When you look closely, it becomes clear why the front-line sales manager role is one of the most challenging in corporations today.

Figure 13-1. Sales Management System

Entire books have been dedicated to sales management, and this system could easily become one. I will do my best to explain the system in one chapter while giving you enough information to understand and build the system.

Remove Barriers to FLSM Engagement

This is a major key to success for front-line sales managers (FLSM). As such, it's worth calling out in the system as something that requires thought and focus.

I once consulted with a company whose leaders asked me to teach their managers to coach. I asked how they knew the managers weren't coaching, and they told me that they had just conducted a 360-degree evaluation and a large majority of sales reps indicated they were not receiving coaching from their managers. I asked to speak with the managers and conducted a focus group, where I quickly learned why they weren't coaching: Company leaders had put far too many low-value requirements on their FLSMs, preventing them from spending time with their team to diagnose performance gaps and deliver the field training and coaching needed to improve performance. It's hard to imagine, given that this is the real job of a front-line sales manager, but I see it all the time.

When the barriers were removed, and we further honed the managers' ability to coach effectively, the gains were tremendous. Very often, we need to start by getting out of the "sales prevention business," or in this case, the "coaching prevention business." That's what this first step is all about.

Take a hard look at the expectations that are set for your FLSMs (or set them clearly, if you haven't yet), what success should look like, and what barriers your leadership team is tossing in their way that prevent FLSMs from doing high-value activities with their team. Remove as many barriers as possible. Then ensure that managers focus their new-found time on those high-value activities—many of which are other components in this system.

Sales Hiring

Sales hiring (also known as talent acquisition or sales selection) is its own system, detailed in building block 4. The science and processes in this system provide the potential for great success. You will only realize that potential, however, if you use the system to customize an effective hiring process and consistently execute it well. The front-line sales managers are the enablers or barriers to success for this system, which is why it's included here in the Sales Management System.

To be clear, managers are only peripherally involved in the creation of the system. Their feedback can be constructive when creating job profiles, determining competencies and traits, and creating situations or case studies for testing hypothetical judgment or skill validations and simulations. At the same time, manager opinions and gut-feel should not override the science you are trying to implement or anything that is based on research and data.

The FLSM's responsibility is the execution of their parts of the system. They:

- Review results of psychometric assessments to prep for interviews.
- Conduct behavioral interviews and ask whatever hypothetical or judgment questions you have developed.
- Lead or participate in the simulations, including scoring them.
- Make some reference calls (perhaps sales manager to former sales manager calls, although many companies outsource this or have talent acquisition team members do it instead).
- Participate in interviewer feedback calibration sessions to understand each interviewer's perspective and make a final hiring determination.

To get this right, get your FLSMs engaged, bought-in, and executing effectively. The payoffs are significant.

Sales Management Operating System

The specific activities in the sales management operating system (smOS), and the rhythm or cadence at which they recur, may vary from company to company based on a variety of factors (sales nuances). I've tried to select components that are as universal as possible, but as always, use good judgment about what is right for your business.

In Figure 13-1, think of:

- The operating system (on the left) as the placeholder for the activities managers consistently do and the cadence for how often those things occur.
- The Sales Process, Sales Methodology, and Customer Lifecycle (in the middle) as the foundation for and context in which the activities to the right occur. Managers must be experts in your process, methodologies, and your customer lifecycle to lead their teams.
- The activities (on the right, from account assignments down through account management) are the things that managers do to execute the smOS. Each activity requires specific expertise to do well, and most are done in recurring meetings with their team or individual team members.

It's important to note that these activities are variable, based on the company. The ones listed in the figure, while common, are intended to be representations, not mandates.

In addition, there are a variety of team and rep meetings, such as:

- A monthly or weekly team meeting
- Individual and team pipeline reviews and forecast meetings
- A recurring team meeting for sharing best practices (often biweekly or monthly; can be standalone or included in another monthly team meeting)
- One-on-one ride-alongs, call-alongs, or call recording reviews
- Individual coaching sessions

As you implement your smOS, your leadership team needs to make decisions about which activities and meetings to include, the best practice they will implement for each, and the regular cadence for each (daily, weekly, biweekly, monthly, or quarterly).

Sales Process

It seems obvious perhaps, but managers must be experts with your sales process and the activities that occur within it. (Surprisingly, many sales managers I speak with can't clearly articulate the difference between process and methodology, so perhaps it isn't as obvious as it might seem.) Sales process represents the stages an opportunity progresses through to a buying decision (see building block 7).

The sales process is like any other process documentation. It includes the process stages (in this case, the stages a sale moves through), the objectives of each stage, the tasks performed in each, and the desired outcomes of each (sometimes referred to as verifiable outcomes). When it's properly aligned to the buying process, the sales process will also include the buying process exit criteria.

The sales process should be a response to the customer lifecycle and buying process, not a rigid, inside-out process that reps follow robotically. As mentioned, your sales process should not only be aligned to the buying process, but also document the buying process exit criteria. This alignment and documentation work isn't performed by sales managers, but must be well understood and executed by them through their sales teams.

FLSMs should ensure that reps are identifying where buyers are in their buying process, responding appropriately, and documenting the opportunity record effectively in your CRM. This is essentially what I mean by "sales process" in the smOS; I'll detail other aspects as we progress through the activity components.

Opportunity qualification, opportunity management, and pipeline management are also closely related to the sales process, but I'm choosing to call them out separately as activities that occur within the sales process, sales methodology, and customer lifecycle.

Sales Methodology

Sales methodology represents the buyer- or customer-facing selling tasks that occur in a sales process (see chapter 9). It's what the reps do in each stage of the sales process that is related to sales skills—the frameworks, models, skills, competencies, and behaviors they use while navigating through the process with their buyers. It does not include all process tasks, because not all process tasks are buyer-facing or selling skills. Whatever sales methodology (or methodologies) you use, your FLSMs must:

- Be experts at it.

- Recognize when reps are or aren't using it (their selling activities—what they are doing and how much).
- Determine to what degree they are or aren't using it (the quality of the activities).
- Be able to coach reps to higher levels of skill performance, which should lead to better sales results.

Methodology ties back to the Sales Readiness System (where it is applied) and the Sales Training System (where it is taught, sustained, transferred, and coached to mastery), so I won't detail it further here. By placing it here, I am simply suggesting that FLSMs must understand the methodology's best practices and be able to diagnose, train, coach, and support the chosen sales methodology.

Customer Lifecycle

As with your sales process and sales methodology, your front-line sales managers must understand your customer lifecycle, work with it, and be able to train reps to adapt to it. For more on customer lifecycle, review chapter 8.

Account Assignments and Territory Optimization

Whatever your organization does to analyze account and territory potential and assign accounts and territories to your sales reps, your sales managers must understand your organization's approach to territory optimization and be able to guide their teams to maximize their account assignments and territories.

Quota and Goal Setting

Front-line sales managers may not approve the final quotas, but at a minimum should be involved with the process to ensure quotas are attainable for their team. They may also be involved in spreading their division or region quota equitably across territories.

Lead Management

Much of lead management is dependent on the sales role being supported, how the marketing team is handling demand generation, whether there is a sales development team, and other factors. This makes it difficult to recommend a universal model. It doesn't matter how your company drives leads or involves your sales force in lead generation, prospecting, and lead management; your FLSMs must be experts at anything reps are expected to do so they can assess, field train, and coach them accordingly.This might include things like:

- Social research, social marketing, and social nurturing
- Territory, account, and contact research
- Using alerts or social listening tools to monitor for trigger events and sales signals
- Taking marketing or sales development rep (SDR) hand-offs and following up quickly yet effectively
- Qualifying leads
- Entering leads and opportunities appropriately in your CRM
- Using the supporting sales engagement and sales enablement tools (a separate component, but it applies here)

Opportunity Qualification

Whatever you call it (lead, deal, sales, or opportunity qualification), and whatever qualification system you use (there are many), being able to train, coach, and manage a qualification method is a key component of sales management.

There are some obvious crossovers between this skill and pipeline management (sometimes still referred to as funnel management), opportunity management, and forecast management, but I believe that qualifying is so important and so often done poorly that it deserves to be called out and addressed specifically. Expert qualification solves so many downstream problems with sales process and forecast management that every company should prioritize it.

If you are not already, consider using an opportunity scoring system for qualification and capture, and track it in your CRM to create visibility and foster accountability.

Opportunity Management

Opportunity management is the effective application of your sales methodologies to an opportunity in your pipeline, which allows you to manage that opportunity through your sales process stages to a successful outcome.

To me, the hidden magic of opportunity management is uncovering the buying process exit criteria for each buyer or decision maker and meeting those criteria to gain continual commitments to move forward. (As a reminder, buying process exit criteria include anything a buyer needs to see, hear, feel, understand, or believe in the stage they're in to feel comfortable moving forward to the next stage with you.)

Pipeline Management

As mentioned earlier, many of these components intertwine. Pipeline management is linked to sales process, sales methodology, opportunity qualification, and forecast management.

Opportunity management refers to managing a single opportunity through the sales process. Pipeline management refers to appropriately managing multiple opportunities (your entire pipeline) to meet your predetermined goals and quotas. It's how you fill your pipeline and conduct opportunity management on a larger scale.

FLSMs must be experts in pipeline management, conducting pipeline review sessions, and training, guiding, and coaching reps to expertly manage their own pipelines. Combine this with opportunity qualification and your pipeline health will improve dramatically (as will your forecast). I see this as a simple truth about selling that is often overlooked or done poorly. Each rep must manage their own pipeline effectively, which rolls up to the manager's divisional or regional pipeline.

Forecast Management

Forecasting accurately is a major pain point in many companies. Countless books, e-books, briefs, whitepapers, articles, and blog posts have been written about this discipline. Software products and companies exist with the sole purpose of better supporting a company's forecasting effort. Yet research and company performances worldwide continually show that many can't do this well. Mostly that's because they haven't done the other things well up to this point.

Great forecast management is a culmination of doing other things well. If you do, forecasts improve. Sound opportunity qualification, sales process alignment, great pipeline management, and the effective execution of your sales methodology will yield higher-quality opportunities with more accurate assessments of their statuses. This means that opportunities will be more predictable than average, yielding far better than the low level of forecasting accuracy we see today.

Managers must be experts in forecasting, and guide reps to do what's necessary to allow them to forecast well. If you fix the other things, forecasting will improve. Pushing for weekly or month-end updates from reps to meet a forecast need, and then fudging most of that data or applying random filters to what you do or don't believe will not result in an accurate forecast. (Although I bet I could sell a lot of Magic 8-Balls at month's end if I tried.)

Account Management

Again, here's some overlap. The skills of account management are part of the sales methodology. This is what sales reps do. The management of the process and implementation of account planning and strategic account management are part of what the sales managers do.

In many companies, account management is thin, at best. I see a dramatic lack of sales call objectives (and back-up objectives), call plans, account objectives, SWOT analyses, force-field analyses, and well-constructed account plans. When there are plans, they often sit unused on a shelf, in a drawer, or in a digital file. There is a marked absence of gathering, sharing, and using account intelligence, and a deficiency in many other aspects of strategic account management. Far too many sales methodologies are incomplete, focusing on subsets of selling, while missing the importance of end-to-end customer lifecycle management.

Managers must be experts here as well and guide their teams toward far better account management practices.

Team and Rep Meetings

Sales managers should lead various team and individual meetings in some predetermined cadence. These vary by company, so you should determine which meetings are right for you, decide on the best practices for each, establish an expected cadence, and execute consistently. For example, these meetings could include:

- A weekly, biweekly, or monthly team meeting (or short weekly meetings and a longer, more robust monthly meeting)
- Biweekly pipeline meetings with the team
- Weekly individual pipeline and performance review meetings
- End of month (EOM) and end of quarter (EOQ) forecasting meetings (separate from pipeline management)
- Performance observations—such as sales call listen-ins (live or call recordings) or field meeting ride-alongs (live in-person, live virtual, or call recordings)—and the resulting field training and coaching follow-up sessions

- Best-practice sharing or team training meetings
- Virtual coaching tools (which you should be using) in an established cadence or ad-hoc as needed.

Sales Coaching Framework

Sales Analytics and ROAM

It almost seems as if we expect that FLSMs will understand how to pull, review, interpret, and use sales analytics through osmosis or magic; but it doesn't work that way. Many managers don't really understand what I call "sales math" (what the numbers really mean, and how to diagnose their reps' performance gaps).

Most people who move into sales management roles from front-line sales roles haven't given much consideration to how activity metrics, leading and lagging indicators, and other reporting have a dot-connection to skills and behaviors, or how the analytics can be used to diagnose areas for improvement.

If you don't offer such training for your sales managers, you should. Stop believing in magic.

ROAM is a sales diagnostic model that helps managers know where to focus coaching efforts for the best return and how to dissect what's not working to fix it. (See building block 6.) The acronym stands for:

- **Results** versus **Objectives** (comparing objectives to identify gaps or shortfalls in results)
- **Activity** (review what reps are doing, with whom, how much, and, as applicable, when and where)
- **Methodology** (determine the quality of the activity, or how well they're executing the sales methodology)

I first used the method (originally as RAM) with great results in 2004, as part of a program I designed called Partnership Coaching. I've used it many times since and have never seen it fail when executed well.

I added objectives in 2016 to remind users that we need to start by not just reviewing results, but comparing them to the intended objectives. This helps managers identify shortfalls and areas on which to focus. As surprisingly simple as that seems, many managers don't have a plan for where to start coaching purposefully. Usually, it's opportunistic or happenstance, which means that the resulting "coaching" is simply very directive feedback.

Performance Analysis and Solutions

I also address this in the chapter on sales coaching. You can use the conditions, reasons, and solutions for performance chart (Figure 7-4), adapted from Ferdinand Fournies' work, to explain the causes of performance issues and identify the appropriate times to use training, coaching, and other solutions.

Field Training and Coaching

Field training and coaching aren't rocket science. It just takes a top-down commitment to the need, a willingness to remove barriers, teaching these simple methods, setting up a system to capture coaching and track results, and the willingness to hold managers accountable for doing it. See chapter 7.

Sales Performance Management

Part of sales performance management is embedded in the building block for sales training with the Sales Training System (to perpetuate skills taught and cement change in the culture). Managers must excel at this. If we know the behaviors that produce results for reps, reps should be held to that standard (for the activities, methodologies, and results), and their performance should be managed accordingly. The same is true for front-line sales managers. Performance management should be a cultural expectation that is applied with positive, helpful intention as part of the fabric of the sales organization.

Lest it seem unfair that the sales organization is managed so rigorously, perhaps even beyond any other function, remember this: Other departments can add tremendous value to clients and the organization. Other departments can create risk for the organization or take it down (for example, mismanaged accounting is a nightmare). But with the possible exception of marketing (with the growing emphasis on demand generation, ABM, and marketing-driven revenue attribution), there is no other department or function that can save the company if sales does not perform.

Nothing happens until somebody sells something. (If you prefer a more buyer-centric perspective, nothing happens until somebody buys something—but either way, a sale is made). So, treat your sales team well, encourage engagement, listen to and solve their problems, and invest in infrastructure that supports them and their training and development. Do all of that. But also manage their performance and hold them accountable with sales performance management. Front-line sales managers must know how to do this and do it well.

But today, sales performance management is even more than that. Gartner (2018) describes SPM solutions as:

> A suite of operational and analytical functions that automate and unite back-office operational sales incentives processes. SPM is implemented to improve sales execution and operational efficiency. Capabilities include:
>
> - Sales incentive compensation management (ICM)
> - Objectives management
> - Quota management and planning
> - Territory management and planning
> - Advanced analytics (benchmarking, predictive and prescriptive, and machine learning/cognitive)
> - Gamification

The most powerful statement in Gartner's report speaks to the potential of SPM, the supporting software, and why everyone should be considering it:

> SPM accelerates representatives' time to value by providing real-time visibility into pay and performance. It provides opportunity estimation of expected commissions, thus encouraging sales representatives to keep more accurate forecasting in the CRM system, and provides motivation for increased close rates on profitable sales. SPM, bridged with CRM, raises execution results of companies' go-to-market efforts with the execution of more effective compensation plans at the territory and field representative levels. (Gartner 2018)

At a minimum, we must have front-line sales managers actively engaged in pipeline management, forecasting, rep performance management, and sales analytics with the corresponding field training and coaching. At best, it's also time to explore the possibilities that SPM software can offer to further support your managers and sales force.

Sales and Management Technology

I can't tell you how many times I've worked at companies where the managers barely knew how to use the CRM system or other sales support technology and needed constant assistance. When that happened, expecting them to be able

Figure 13-2. Sales Management System

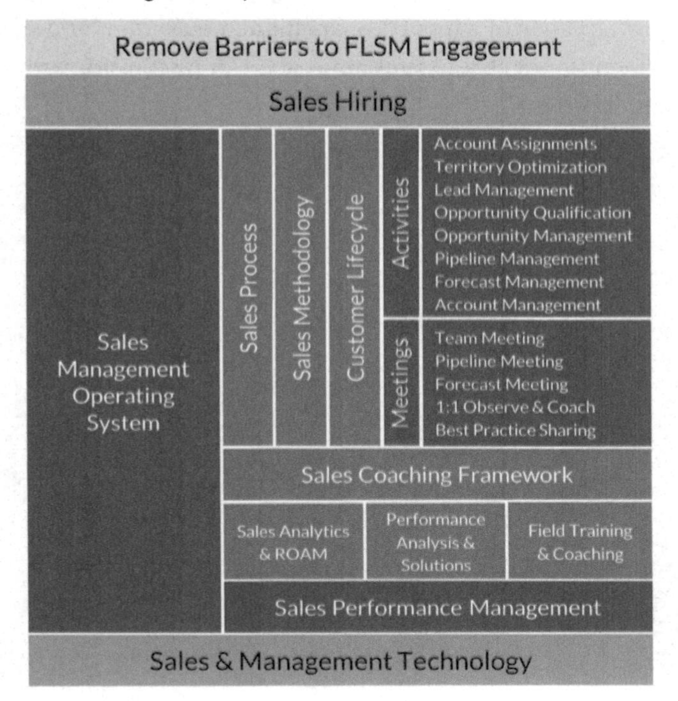

to explain why the sales enablement tools were needed and how to use them effectively was a lost cause. (See chapter 11.)

Front-line sales managers must get a handle on technology and master it. We're in the 21st century. Rolodexes, card files, and doing everything manually are practices of a bygone era.

Make the expectations crystal clear and give managers a rationale and ROI case, the training, the practice, and the support they require to maximize these tools and help their reps do the same.

Summary

This chapter is devoted to the Sales Management System and its many components. While it's more complex than the previous systems we've discussed, its value to the success of your sales managers is enormous. Sales managers need a solid foundation for setting expectations and goals, active listening and communication skills, and leading meetings effectively, as well as any other skills required for performance management. While the nuances of the system might be challenging, sales managers usually grasp them quickly, when explained. Then, it's just a matter of supporting disciplined execution and mastery. It is no overstatement to say this systems approach can be transformative to a sales management effort.

14 Communication Management

Sales Force and Cross-Functional Collaborators

Aside from being a Pink Floyd reference, I use the phrase "bricks in the wall" to refer to all the other corporate functions and departments that sales enablement practitioners collaborate with to support sales force performance (Figure 14-1).

Figure 14-1. Sales Enablement Collaborators—the Bricks in the Wall

Cross-Functional Collaboration

Sales Development
Demand Generation
Field Sales
Product Marketing
Sales Operations
Marketing Operations
Customer Success
Legal
Human Resources
Finance
Training
IT

I don't see communication management as a building block, per se. I view it as a practice, along with systems thinking, that supports the other building blocks and ties them together.

People occasionally want to debate this with me, and if it seems important to them, I give up easily. Call it a building block if you'd like. I love a good debate, but as my friend and colleague Doug Wyatt often says, this isn't "the hill I want to die on." (Remember: The map is not the territory.)

Here's what is important.

Centralized Communication With the Sales Force

Sellers can be easily overwhelmed and confused if their leaders are constantly communicating with them through various sources. It's worse when they or their managers can't locate information when it's needed because it was sent from various parties, delivered in multiple ways, or buried in email or deleted. The sales enablement function can reduce or eliminate this distraction by:

- Becoming the single point of communication for the sales force (with the possible exceptions of the senior sales leader and CEO)
- Communicating with a regular cadence (with exceptions for emergencies or opportunity win announcements, if you do those)
- Using a consistent, well-organized communications format
- Storing communications in a centralized place where the sales force can always find and search for them

None of this is difficult—the most challenging can be getting top-down support and agreement from other functions that want to communicate directly with the sales force. The benefits of raising the importance of their communication, the likelihood of it being consumed, and the ability to find it when needed, will hopefully outweigh any concerns.

In terms of platforms for communications or storage and retrieval, organizations can use:

- An information storage and retrieval system
- A knowledge management system
- Digital document management software
- Their sales enablement software or learning experience platforms
- A wiki
- A simple, searchable intranet site with dated links to each weekly or biweekly communication (similar to a blog)

Communication format is another important consideration. An instructional designer, communications expert, or someone familiar with information mapping will be able to help you organize a reusable format that makes it easier for readers to absorb and retain the information. Sometimes, answering the simple who, what, why, how, when, and where questions will suffice, although I do highly recommend exploring information mapping. You'll be surprised what you can apply to your training design, documentation design, and communication.

Ongoing Communication With Collaborators and Stakeholders

This is the second critical chunk of communication management for sales enablement. You should establish a cadence of meetings and communication with:

- Your manager and team colleagues (you're probably already doing this)
- Your cross-functional collaboration partners
- Your executive team and other leadership stakeholders

Your meetings, topics, and communication with these teams, as well as the cadence of communication, may vary based on how you are collaborating with them. Speaking generally, you will want to review collaboration efforts, progress reports, results, and issues, and then revise your plans or charter as needed. The frequency could be weekly, biweekly, monthly, or quarterly.

For example, you'll want to discuss content use with product marketing and marketing. You might start simply by discussing which content is or isn't being used by the sales force, or even when used doesn't seem to be effective with your buyers. Eventually, when you have enough data to do regression analysis, you may want to do more in-depth studies to learn which content—used when and with whom—correlates with positive outcomes (such as forward movement through the sales process or win rates).

You'll want to have similar conversations with other collaborators in your company, whoever they may be. Laying the foundation for these collaborations and ongoing communication should be part of your sales enablement charter, which is discussed in chapter 16, "How to Get Started."

Summary

Communication management could easily be considered its own building block, but I see it more as a key supportive element for both systems thinking and building block execution. You are communicating with two critical groups here: your sales force and everyone else (that is, colleagues, collaborators, and stakeholders). Both groups require responsive and regular communication through meeting schedules and notifications, and some of these you've likely already established or experienced. It's important to remember how a reliable informational network, cross-functional collaboration, stakeholder alignment, and clear communication can be foundational to building and sustaining team and organizational relationships.

15 Sales Support Services

Over the years, I've seen companies offer a variety of support services for their sales forces. Sometimes these services are provided by sales operations, marketing operations, sales administration, or even sales training functions. If your company has the budget, resources, and desire to offer sales support services, it can make sense to coordinate them as a sales enablement service.

Here is a sampling of what I've seen offered.

Overlay and SME Resources

This is one of the more common services (and may not need to be coordinated by sales enablement if other departments are providing the services).

Overlay and SME (subject matter expert) support refers to a sales specialist role. An account executive or account manager may involve this role to support a client either in a buying process or in implementing a solution, in which case the customer service or customer success department may be requesting the support. Typically, these sales specialists have deep knowledge and experience in their specialty. It's common in sales where the problem or solution is complex or highly technical (such as enterprise software) or highly engineered or manufactured products (such as medical devices, healthcare equipment, oil rigging equipment, or Internet of Things edge computing sensors). In some cases, organizations segment their sales force into highly educated sales specialists who are dedicated to a product line, but an overlay SME is often used.

These specialists may include:

- Sales engineers
- Solution architects
- Product management team members
- Engineering or R&D team members
- A temporary team of specialists for a newly launched, complex product line

The best value that sales enablement can provide is to ensure the process for requesting or scheduling overlay support is the same as for other services, for consistency, and that the sales force understands the requirements and process for requesting support, and follows both.

Account Research Services

Research services could include industry, market, company, or contact research. We say that sales reps don't spend enough time selling or with customers, so this is a service to reduce their nonselling time and help them better prepare for prospecting or meetings with key buyers or customers. Once the industry and market information is captured (or purchased), it just needs to be updated periodically. The company and contact information will evolve more rapidly.

Meeting Preparation Services

In a similar vein, some companies provide meeting preparation support, including not only the necessary research but also coordinating schedules and other meeting logistics. The specific services may vary between in-person meetings and web conferences, but research, preparation, logistics, and coordination are required for each.

Presentation Support Services

Presentation support includes the design or compiling of presentation resources for a specific meeting. In most cases, it would likely require the customization of templates, but could also mean support for the design and development of presentation materials.

RFP Support Services

In industries and companies where RFPs (request for proposal) or RFIs (request for information) are common, it often makes more sense to centralize the responses with a group that has the correct information and messaging and a history of responding in the most effective way, than to dole them out to sales reps. Once the buying committee is ready to engage with a sales professional, the process can be turned over. (In some cases, if it's a highly valuable strategic client, the RFP team might involve a rep to attempt to break through the request veil to shape buyer perceptions or influence the RFP, but the success of this sort of effort is variable, based on the purchasing company's policies, and does come with some risk.)

Deal Desk Services

A "deal desk" is a group of internal experts who are assembled to review and provide feedback on the pursuit of high-value sales opportunities to improve the chance of winning the business. Some deal desks are static, meaning they comprise a group of preselected experts who meet periodically to review submitted opportunities (although they may include others by invite, as needed). Others are assembled on a deal-by-deal basis, depending on the circumstances and the details of the specific opportunity. In some cases, deal desk members may be used to help architect a complex solution or construct an appropriate and effective proposal and agreement.

Coaching Services

This service is fairly self-explanatory; however, you might offer coaching services for your front-line sales managers as well as your sellers or sales support specialists.

I strongly believe it is the front-line sales managers' responsibility to coach their sales reps. That said, I recognize that there are times when managers may need the support, and times when coaching reps directly may be appropriate. These include:

- In a startup where the front-line sales manager (FLSM) must be a seller-manager. (This is not something I usually support, but it's also a real-world nuance that we need to acknowledge in startups.)
- When a rapidly growing business is hiring and onboarding more sales reps than an FLSM could possibly support while also leading and managing their current team.
- In very small organizations, less complex companies, or those with simple sales processes or other situations where sales enablement does not require as much dedicated time and can assist with field coaching

without detracting from influencing organization-wide sales force performance. (However, even in this case, I believe they should work with or through the FLSM.)

- On an as-needed, occasional basis when the FLSM needs help with a particular sales rep and the enablement leader has the specific or deeper expertise needed to help.
- When an FLSM is being coached and supported on how to coach reps more effectively. (Again, this should be on an as-needed, occasional basis.)

With such exceptions noted, using sales enablement staff or others to coach reps directly on a more permanent basis is generally the completely wrong approach toward sales enablement. Peer coaching, coaching from company executives, external coaching, or cross-team coaching (swapping managers) are creative options to consider in developmental plans, but they're not a replacement for the manager-rep coaching relationship.

Manager coaching is an entirely different story. Investing time to better train, prepare, enable, and empower front-line sales managers is one of the smartest investments a business can make. Whether it's you or your enablement team, or you engage an external expert, coaching managers can deliver a significant ROI. This is especially true if you are implementing a coaching program and expect your managers to effectively coach your reps, or if you are implementing a new sales process, sales methodology, or sales management operating system with a cadence.

Requesting Services

So, how can people make these service requests? From what I've seen it varies, but they're often offered through service-level agreements (SLAs). These agreements are a commitment between the service provider (in this case, sales enablement or the functions mentioned earlier) and the receiver of the service (in our case, the sales organization). Particular aspects of the service—when and how to request services, prerequisites, information that must be provided, the level of service, availability, and responsibilities—are documented and agreed on between the service provider and the service user.

In some cases—due to the costs involved and the increase in expenses—companies will outsource to service providers on an as-needed basis or consider offshore resources.

Summary

Sales support services include operations that could be provided through sales enablement by the variety of functions that support sales; for example, services for presentation and meeting preparation, account research, manager coaching, and subject matter expertise. These could be needed in startup capacities or for rapidly growing businesses. For sales success, it's important to understand and monitor what your sales force requires in the way of sales support.

16

How to Get Started

Remember the old joke about how to get to Carnegie Hall? The surprise answer was "practice, practice, practice."

Imagine if you really had to answer that question, in the absence of GPS technology. It'd be important to know your friend's starting point, right? In my webinars, I use this cartoon to illustrate the point relative to how to start or evolve a sales enablement function.

Develop a Sales Enablement Charter

I'm a big fan of alignment. A boat won't go as fast as possible if the rowers are paddling in opposite directions. Long before I heard others talk about developing a "sales enablement charter," I just called it a strategic and tactical plan for my department. Whatever words you use, you need one.

Developing your charter is about getting clarity, establishing priorities, setting expectations, implementing measuring systems, and creating plans. Once your charter is in place it will foster alignment, provide clarity, and get you all rowing in the same direction. When there is conflict or things veer off track, you can refer back to the charter, which will either get you back in alignment, identify a need to escalate the issue for a decision, or uncover the need for a charter update.

Table 16-1 is the simple framework I share with those who want to start right—with a charter.

Table 16-1. Simple Framework With Charter

Why	Why are you starting or evolving your sales enablement function?
What	• How will you define sales enablement? • If starting, where will you start? If evolving, what will you change or add? • What roles will you support? (For example, AE, AM, SDR, BDM, sales engineer, FLSM, channel partner, or other) • Which building blocks will you support? • What issues or performance problems will you address? • What outcomes will you deliver?
Who	• Who is going to do it? • Where or to whom will this function report? • With whom (what other functions or leaders) will you collaborate?
How	• How will this work be done and to what level? • How will the work or desired outcomes be prioritized and measured? • How will you collaborate and communicate with your internal partners and report results?

In this example, I used the simple questions of why, what, who, and how, and worked within that framework. If you want, you can always opt for more businesslike and detailed terms like purpose, objectives, inputs, tasks, plans, outputs, deliverables, stakeholders, collaborators, outcomes, metrics, or time-line. What's important is that you create a framework and build a plan that makes sense for you and your collaborators, and, more critically, will be respected, accepted, and used in your company culture.

Whichever plan structure you use, start with why (or whatever you call it). Why are you starting or evolving your sales enablement function? What is the purpose? Get alignment on this with your leadership team and collaborators, and it will serve you well and remove a lot of friction as you execute your plans.

Conduct a Current–Future State Gap and Impact Analysis

As a fan of data-driven decision making and performance consulting, I like to start with diagnostics, and encourage the same. There are many terms for this, so if you're familiar with a training needs analysis, front-end analysis, or gap analysis (the A in the ADDIE model—analyze, design, development, implement, and evaluate), this is similar. I like to imagine I'm conducting discovery for my own sales force—as if I'm selling sales performance improvement services (which is basically what we do in sales enablement).

In SPARXiQ's Modern Sales Foundations course, we teach my situation assessment framework using COIN-OP (Table 16-2).

Table 16-2. COIN-OP Framework

What is the current state and the impact of doing nothing?	• Consider the challenges, opportunities, and impacts of the current state (COI)
What is the desired future state (the desired outcomes and priority of those outcomes)?	• Consider the needs, outcomes, and priorities of the future state (NOP)
Impact Analysis	• Can you quantify or "dollarize" the gap?
Gap Analysis	• What will it take to close the gap? • What needs to change?
Force Field Analysis	• What factors or forces are helping push you toward your desired future state? • What factors or forces are holding you back or hindering your progress?

I find this framework very helpful, whether I'm conducting a situation assessment during sales discovery or assessing the situation for performance improvement potential. The impact analysis will help you create a business case for change, while the gap analysis will help you determine what to focus on to support your sales leaders in achieving their goals for the sales force.

Use the Building Blocks and Systems as Diagnostic Tools

You can also layer the situation assessment framework with COIN-OP into your existing analysis. As you're doing your current state to future state analysis, simply assess your current practices in each of the building blocks or sales systems versus where you want to be. This can help you prioritize the building blocks to make them less overwhelming. (I'm obviously writing a book about the building blocks and believe they're an excellent framework, but I also recognize that considering a dozen blocks, with systems, communication, and support services can feel a little like trying to eat an elephant.)

Create a Measurement and Evaluation Strategy That Works

Given the charter with outcomes, and your impact and gap analysis, you should already have a clear idea of the metrics that you need to evaluate progress. In a sales organization, you're likely already measuring these in some way, but you may want to consider leading indicators that forecast your progress, as well as the lagging indicators that prove it. This will allow you to pivot and adjust along the way as needed.

In addition to the measures, consider how, when, and to whom you will report progress, especially with your aligned collaborators and stakeholders. This will allow you to assess together, pivot together, and celebrate together.

Summary

This short chapter helps you start analyzing your sales enablement function with frameworks of prompts and questions to apply some of the analytical tools I've introduced in earlier chapters.

17 A Performance-Based Approach to Sales Onboarding

Sales onboarding always seems to be a hot topic. How do we get our new salespeople onboarded and up to speed as quickly as possible? It's a question that every sales leader asks and, sooner or later, something every sales enablement leader faces.

I cut my teeth in sales enablement (called sales training at the time) when I joined a corporate training department in 1991 and took over a rather lackluster sales onboarding program. The program I designed and implemented became legendary in that company. The whole experience was a learning lab for me, where I experimented with everything I was absorbing through reading and my successful experience as a seller and manager. Eventually, the program was producing new employees with 120 days on the job (90 days post-graduation) who were outperforming a control group of five-year employees.

I've repeated that experience multiple times in multiple companies, and it's led to many of the things I've shared in this book. You can have the same experience, and it's my hope that this book will shorten your journey to mastery and impact. To get started, you need an understanding of why training typically fails to produce the intended results, as well as some common onboarding program challenges.

Why does training fail to produce intended results?

- Poor hiring and selection practices
- Training is not the right solution for the performance problem
- Training is the right solution, but the training content does not get results when used
- The instructional design is weak, resulting in a poor learner experience
- There is no knowledge sustainment plan to foil the forgetting curve
- There is too little skill development (practice) with feedback loops
- There is no purposeful transfer plan to help reps apply what they learned
- Managers do not coach their reps to achieve skill mastery
- There is no measurement plan to assess the effectiveness or allow pivots
- The expected behaviors for the role are not incorporated into the company's performance management approach
- There is no aligned change management plan

Common challenges in sales onboarding programs include:

- There is no logical plan
- There is no defined difference between pre-boarding, orientation, and sales onboarding (which is the job-related knowledge and skills training required to enable new hires for sales success)
- Combining pre-boarding, orientation, and onboarding, because an uncoordinated effort derails the onboarding
- Too much training content is delivered too quickly and too soon
- An endless parade of presentations from SMEs
- Event-based approaches that are in-person or virtual boot camps with no follow-up or continued tracking toward milestones
- No checkpoints, gating, assessments, skill validations, or certifications (what do they know or what can they do?)
- No sustainment, skill development, transfer, or coaching plans
- Reps are not taught using a simulated sales process workflow, from left to right (that is, how to actually do their job, on the first day back)
- "Go get 'em, tiger!" is the prevailing attitude; meaning, we hired experienced people, gave them some product training, and now they need to "get to it" and "go sell something." (This always reminds me of the old saying in the field of emergency management: "Meet 'em, greet 'em, treat 'em, and street 'em!")

Let's explore these ideas in more detail.

Get Sales Hiring Right

Hiring right is the first step of successful onboarding. For more on this, see building block 4, sales hiring (as well as the Sales Hiring System).

Stop the Madness (Avoid Failure)

Review the list of reasons for training failure and common sales onboarding challenges. Assess your program honestly against these challenges and plan how to address them. If you are creating a new sales onboarding program, build it with these challenges in mind and work to purposefully avoid them. Sometimes it's just as valuable to know what *not* to do or what to avoid.

Start Doing Things Differently to Ensure Success

Stopping the madness is the first step. It's necessary, but it's not sufficient. If you want to radically improve your sales onboarding outcomes, you also need to start doing things differently:

- Ensure you're teaching content that matters and will get results in the real world.
- Set performance milestones that progressively move the reps toward acceptable levels of performance.
- Prioritize the need-to-know content and teach it by milestone.
- Chunk, sequence, and layer your content for better absorption and retention.
- Use process and workflow to teach reps how to actually do their job. (Don't teach randomly organized content, even if it's chunked, sequenced, and layered.)
- Maximize modern learning methods for efficiency and effectiveness.
- Support your onboarding program with systems thinking.

Use Top-Producer Analysis or Proven Content

Conducting research with your own top producers is a great way to ensure that the content you teach will get results. If you go this route, here's a crash course on top-producer analysis (TPA):

- Conduct task analyses as you would for a training project. Think back to what you learned about sales process stages (objectives, tasks, and exit criteria). Focus on the tasks.
- Examine what top producers do, why they do it, how they do it, when it seems to matter, and when and where they do it. Examine the activities

they perform and the sales methods they use. Capture their workflow. Define how top producers manage the sales process and incorporate sales methodology.

- Document the difficulty, importance, and frequency of their selling behaviors. This will help your instructional designer.
- When possible, align what your top producers do with your sales competencies, if you have them documented, or update and validate the competencies based on your top-producer analysis.
- Identify the real performance levers (the 20 percent of what they do that delivers 80 percent of their results).
- Study your middle producers in a similar way. Compare top producers to middle producers to find the differentiators.
- Build continue–start–stop lists based on your analysis—what should other performers continue to do, start doing, or stop doing, based on what the top producers do?
- Build your training content around the repeatable, replicable skills of the top producers, focusing on the differentiators.

Of course, if you (or others in your company) don't have the experience, time, resources, or statistical prowess to conduct a top-producer analysis and identify the differentiating skills and behaviors between your top producers and middle producers, there are other options. You can select a proven, effective commercial sales methodology that fits your industry, company, buyers and customers, and solution set. Just keep in mind that many commercial sales methodologies are not complete and do not span the entire customer lifecycle. You may need more than one to supplement what you purchase.

Figure 17-1. Top Producers

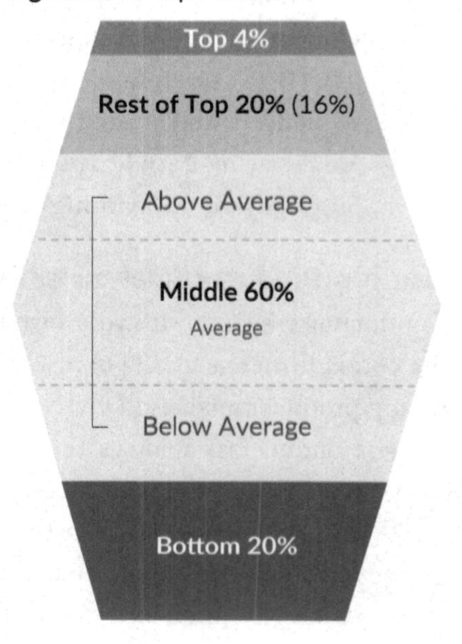

Set Performance Milestones

Determine major performance milestones for your new hires and document when you think they will be able to achieve them. If you have performance ramp-up data from past new hires, you can use those benchmarks to start, and shorten them over time. Milestones may vary by industry, company, product, service, sales cycle, and quota structure. You need to determine the most reasonable and effective milestones for your company.

Figure 17-2 shows an example of a series of three performance milestones for a company with a short sales cycle and monthly quotas. In a case like this, the milestones are all lagging indicators. (We discussed leading and lagging indicators in the chapter on building block 9: sales analytics and metrics. See that chapter for examples.)

Figure 17-2. Performance Milestones

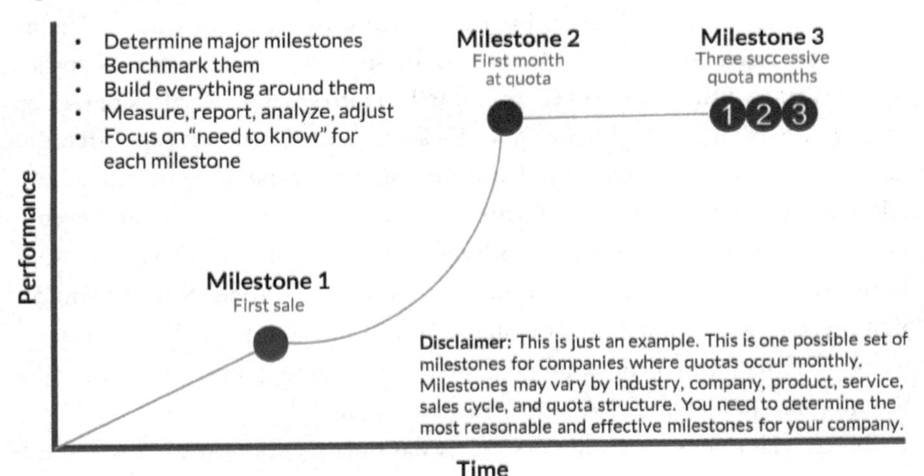

For a company with a longer sales cycle, you need to establish both leading and lagging indicators so you can track progress milestones toward the eventual sale. I've seen up to nine milestones for a company with an 18-month average sales cycle. (Knowing your company's sales velocity metrics can be helpful, as well as understanding the average timing for the progression of an opportunity through your sales process stages. Both will help determine whether your new reps are tracking toward success.)

For sales onboarding, you may want to consider using learning performance metrics and sales performance metrics.

Once you set these performance milestones, benchmark them and build everything around them. The goal of your onboarding program should be to get your reps to their milestones in whatever timeframe you set to achieve them. As mentioned in the chapter on sales compensation, you can establish incentives for both newly hired sales reps and their managers for meeting key performance milestones in certain timeframes.

Focus on Need-to-Know Content by Milestone

You need to have prioritization conversations and determine what reps really need to know in order to hit each of your milestones. Other than establishing the milestones themselves, this is one of the most critical steps you can take to dramatically shorten your onboarding ramp-up times.

This is often a lot harder than it sounds, and it's certainly more difficult than it should be. People, especially subject matter experts, are incredibly invested in their content or functional area and what they believe sales reps should know. I once had a very intense debate with a sales operations leader who insisted that new sales reps learn how to use their digital e-signing software in their first month on the job. He presented an introduction to sales operations during onboarding to highlight the various ways his department supported the sales force, and insisted that reps learn the software at the same time. I should add that the average sales cycle for this company was nine months, and even a fast-moving deal took nearly six months. See the problem there? The e-sign software procedures were clearly not need-to-know at this time. Not to mention that the software was well documented with job aids that walked reps through using it; we had also recently implemented Walk Me to guide reps when using the program in real time. Despite all this, we still had the debate.

That sales operations leader's strategy was the exact opposite of just-in-time content or a milestone-based strategy based on need-to-know status. Cramming everything into the first milestone bucket, whether the content is needed then or not, makes ramp-up times so much longer than they need to be. I suggest involving a good instructional designer with firm "need to know" filters in your discussion. In my webinars and conference presentations on this topic, I usually warn people to be ready for the fistfights. That's hyperbole, but, as I mentioned, there definitely will be some lively debates. Let your milestones be your guide.

When you're establishing a sales onboarding program, you'll want to measure everything you can, report on it, analyze the data, and use what you learn to adjust the program for continuous improvement.

The content type or training topics you teach are variable and company-specific, but this is a good starter list. Determine which apply for your sales reps:

- **Industry:** domain expertise, business acumen, insights
- **Market:** problems, risks, opportunities, implications

- **Customers:** ideal customer profile, buyer personas, buyer's journey
- **Territory and accounts:** accounts, contacts, current state, goals
- **Solutions:** products, services, capabilities, differentiators, value, outcomes
- **Sales process:** stages, objectives, tasks, exit criteria, aligned to the buying process
- **Sales methodology:** sales competencies, training and top-producer practices for lead gen, opportunity management, account management
- **Policy and procedure:** internal departmental collaboration and handoffs, standard operating procedures (SOP), forecasting expectations and process
- **Tools:** CRM, sales enablement tools, analytics, organization, collaboration, collateral, performance support, other systems

A Word About Product Training

Most companies spend far too much training time focused on product details and not nearly enough time teaching how to sell the products. Treat this the same as everything else—stop over-training product. Consider:

- What do reps need to know and do to get to each level and reach each milestone?
- Chunk, sequence, and layer the above and teach appropriately. For highly complex products, plan how you will support reps (for example, using sales engineers, a buddy system, mentors, managers, a deal desk, performance support, or great collateral).
- Get off FAB training (feature, advantage, benefit) quickly and start scenario training. When you use scenario training, you document real and simulated buyer situations and have sales reps determine how to solve these very real problems with their solutions.
- Consider using a buyer-centric messaging matrix (Table 17-1).

Have a Curriculum Design Strategy: Chunk, Sequence, Layer

Chunk, sequence, and layer is a well-known instructional design strategy for organizing large amounts of information to help with absorption and retention. It's perfect to help you maximize your onboarding program.

- Chunk like topics together.
- Teach in bite-sized chunks with reinforcement and assessments to increase retention.

Table 17-1. Buyer-Centric Messaging Matrix

	COIN-OP								
Personas	Challenges Opportunities Impacts Needs[1] Outcomes Priorities	Metrics and How They Are Measured	POSE[2] Value Messaging to Capture Interest Based On ← COIN-OP	Targeted Discovery Approach Based On ← COIN-OP	How to Demo or Present Based On ← COIN-OP	How to Build Solutions to Address ← COIN-OP	Common Concerns and How to Resolve	Competitors and How to Position Against	The Outcomes and Value They Want, and How You Enable Both
Role 1									
Role 2									
Role 3									
etc.									

[1] Needs: Business, experiential, aspirational, and personal

[2] POSE: Problem, outcome, solution, and explore

- Order chunks in a logical sequence that makes it easier for the learner to absorb.
- Layer additional related chunks (or new chunks) on top of already-learned knowledge and skills.

One of the most fascinating oddities about instructional design is that anyone who knows something about anything believes they are qualified to design training for it or teach the topic. If you're not an instructional design expert, my best advice is to hire a real, evidence-based, performance-oriented instructional designer or rent an expert (a contractor or freelancer).

Teach Sales Process and Workflow

This syncs very well with chunk, sequence, and layer. Start by mapping your customer life cycle from lead gen through strategic account management, and then determine where in the life cycle your trainees interact with your buyers and customers.

As a reminder:

- **Sales process** is the stages that an opportunity progresses through to a decision.
- **Sales methodology** is what reps do in each stage and how they sell.

Then, design the training and teach your reps using the business process and workflow, from left to right, just as you expect them to do after training:

- Simulate the real-world activities in your training, following the sales process stages or life cycle.
- Teach the best-practice methodology in each stage.
- Use as much role play and simulation as possible (flipped learning) with learning and practice loops, feedback, and coaching.

Maximize Modern Learning Methods

The human brain evolves very slowly, so the way that people learn does not change rapidly. Technology, however, does advance rapidly, and a growing body of cognitive and evidenced-based learning research helps us understand how to design more effective training. There are proven methods and tools available that, if used wisely, can make your job easier and your training more effective.

Assessments and Personalized Learning Paths

Using competency or psychometric assessments is a great way to survey the current levels of sales competencies in your sales force. This allows you to build personalized learning paths organizationally for reps with similar developmental needs and allows managers and reps to collaborate on individual coaching and development plans.

This strategy can also work very well for onboarding. It's especially easy if you already use a competency-based hiring assessment, as recommended in the chapter on sales hiring. In this case, you already have the data.

Another strategy is to create detailed exams for each of your courses in your onboarding curriculum. If the tests are well-designed (consider expert help—designing valid tests is a science), you can use them to allow reps to "test out" of a subject. This strategy is harder to implement in programs taught in centralized classrooms or with in-person bootcamps. Today's many self-directed learning options, blended learning curricula, and virtual training options make it much easier to personalize learning paths based on individual needs.

Mobile Strategy

This is an access strategy. If you are using online learning, blended curricula, and other virtual training strategies, you can make the learning experience available anywhere, anytime, on any device. For onboarding, or at least for the early portions where your new reps temporarily don't have responsibilities other than learning, it's OK to build content for a larger screen and recommend that to your employees. But even then, and certainly beyond that stage, building for mobile will help with adoption, especially for reinforcement and support.

Asynchronous (Self-Directed) Training

Asynchronous or self-directed training, when well designed, can be excellent prework, primary courseware, or reinforcement and learning support. Using e-learning in this way—as a series of shorter courses with one or few learning objectives—is a good strategy to chunk, sequence, and layer your self-directed training and to mix it up with other learning media to reduce fatigue. It can also provide a way for your learners to test out of topics and leap frog to the next course or curriculum. In that case, microlearning and bite-sized courses can make it "just-for-me" training.

Synchronous Instructor-Led Training

Synchronous instructor-led training can be virtual or classroom-based (vILT or ILT, respectively). In both cases, this medium works well when interaction, discussion, brainstorming, hands-on learning, or application are desired. You can also flip the training by using prework to prepare for the ILT or vILT class with hands-on sessions, exercises, activities, practice, role plays, feedback loops, coaching, re-runs (repeating role plays after feedback), discussion, and more. With improvements in virtual training environments and virtual breakout rooms, if you design appropriately for the environment and train instructors to facilitate effectively, you can accomplish almost anything in a virtual class that you could in a physical classroom. The virtual environment does hamper the age-old practice of tossing candy bars or providing stress toys, but the quality of learning can be as good, or better.

Using Spaced Repetition, Retrieval Learning, and Feedback Loops

We know about the forgetting curve, so why not plan for it? Learning reinforcement platforms excel at this, but there are lower-tech methods that work as well. Spaced repetition (reintroducing content) and retrieval learning or asking questions and using quizzes (to illicit a memory response from learners) are both highly effective reinforcement methods. Get creative. If there is a delay between learning and application, purposefully planning your reinforcement approach is especially important.

Figure 17-3. The Forgetting Curve

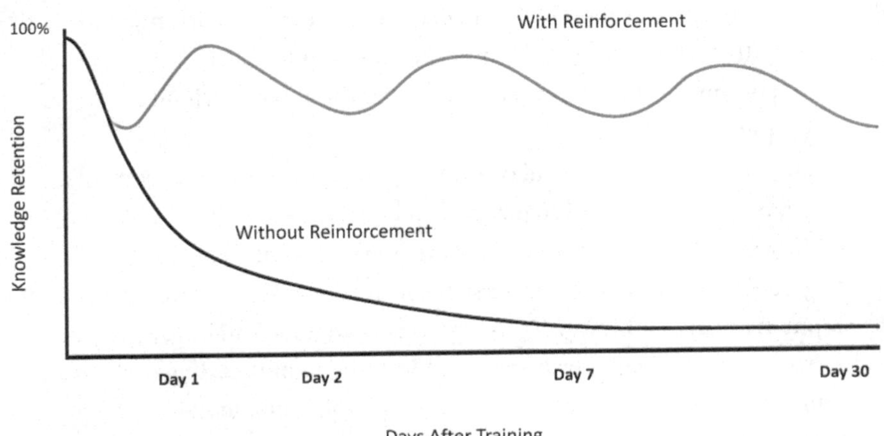

Incorporating Practice With Feedback Loops and Coaching

I mentioned this under synchronous instructor-led training. The programs I've designed that were most effective and produced the best results included the most practice, guiding learners to use skills in the process workflow (as they are expected to work, on-the-job). But then, beyond that, those highly effective programs also incorporated feedback loops and coaching.

Think about the typical sales role play—for a triad role play, there's a sales role, a customer role, and an observer role. All three people have usually just gone through the same training program. At the end of the role play there is a feedback session (often from a fellow trainee). What happens after that? They switch roles and do another role-play exercise. However, there are things you can do to make that role play a lot more valuable:

- Schedule more time so the person who got the feedback can redo the role play, apply the feedback, and then get more feedback.
- Ask others who have previously taken the program, and know how to coach, to play the observer role and provide great feedback.
- Have organization leaders attend and play customers, which makes the customer role much more realistic than when a fellow trainee plays it.

For more role play advice, read these blog posts at mikekunkle.com/blog:

- Sales Leaders: It's Time to Get Serious About Purposeful Practice & Skill Mastery
- Maximizing the Power of Role Play and Sales Simulations

Orchestrating Social and Informal Learning

There is much talk these days about social and informal learning. This is the "20" in the 70-20-10 principle, which posits that people learn:

- 70 percent of their knowledge from on-the-job experience (experiential learning)
- 20 percent through social or informal interactions with others, like peers, colleagues, and managers (informal or social learning)
- 10 percent through formal training events (formal learning)

I agree there is a place for informal learning; it's outstanding for individual development plans. However, if your goal is systematic, orchestrated learning, and a progression through performance milestones in onboarding or measurable performance improvement at the organization level, I remain skeptical that social and informal learning are the right approaches to achieve your desired outcomes.

That said, Figure 17-4 shows some ways it can support your sales onboarding efforts:

- Use a buddy system (with guidelines and training for buddies).
- Orchestrate sharing between your new hires and top producers, SMEs, executives, sales enablers.
- Source and moderate best-practice content.
- Encourage new hires to reflect on their own experiences related to what they are learning now and share their thoughts with their cohorts.
- Try structured OJT to drive better experiential learning with planned outcomes.
- Incorporate social and informal learning throughout the course of everyday work life by including learning huddles, win announcements, sales stories of what worked or didn't and what the rep learned from the experience, or even recordings of well-run live meetings with clients (with permission).

Figure 17-4. Incorporating Informal Learning

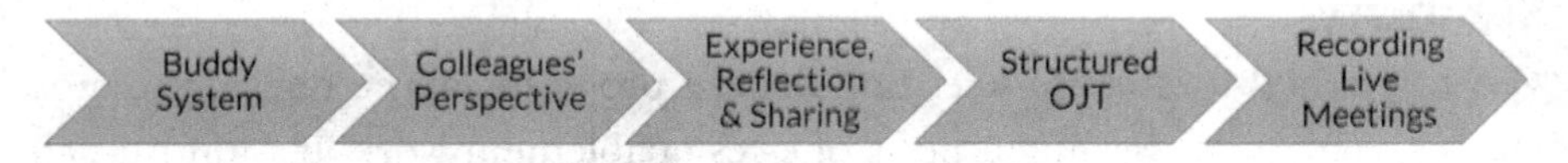

One caution: Ensure you don't have "the blind leading the blind." I once worked for a company that launched a discussion group for their reps to allow them to crowdsource advice from one another. They started the group just before I joined the company. After observing the group for a day, I realized I needed to moderate, because those who needed the help the most were the only ones participating. They were all trying to help each other, but most of their advice was not very helpful. Even worse, since we were in a highly regulated industry, some of their advice was out of compliance (which is what forced me to moderate).

Readiness Validation or Full-Scale Certification

I'm an advocate for readiness validation and even full-scale certification, although I believe the two are often confused, and the latter is seldom really done.

A readiness validation is probably all you need. It is an orchestrated event designed to assess the readiness of your sales onboarding graduates to represent your company and support your customers. It can include written examinations, submitted recordings, live presentations, oral review panels, various role plays and simulations (online and live), or a review of recorded live calls for crucial moments in the sales process (prospecting, discovery, or demo and presentation). It can be a very rigorous process that challenges your learners and validates their readiness.

If you think you want to create a true certification program, I recommend that you pick up Judith Hale's book, *Performance-Based Certification: How to Design a Valid, Defensible, Cost-Effective Program*, and read it from cover to cover. If you still believe you want a full-scale certification, follow her lead.

Execute With Discipline (Using a Systems Approach)

It should come as no surprise that the same systems that support the sales enablement building blocks can also support your sales onboarding program. The advice you need here is already documented elsewhere in this book: See the chapters on the Sales Hiring System, Sales Readiness System, Sales Training System, and the Sales Management System.

Summary

Creating a highly effective sales onboarding program can be one of the most challenging and rewarding aspects of sales enablement work. It's unfortunate that some organizational leaders think this is the only responsibility of sales enablement, perhaps along with product update communication, which confines some enablers to the onboarding and product corner, rather than doing the performance consulting work that could contribute so much more for the sales force. But if you design and develop an onboarding program that truly delivers results, it certainly can open other doors for you. And if you're going to do something, you might as well do it as best you can.

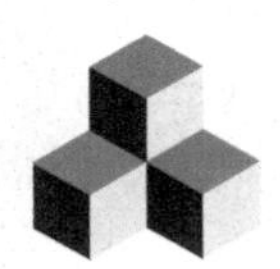

A Look to the Future

Evolving to Sales Performance Consulting

I've been a fan and practitioner of performance consulting for a long time. I read Robert Mager's *The New Mager Six-Pack* and Thomas Gilbert's *Human Competence: Engineering Worthy Performance* for the first time around 1990. After that, I read everything I could get my hands on that was related to performance improvement. I joined ATD (then ASTD) and ISPI (then NSPI). After I read *Handbook of Human Performance Technology*, I was completely hooked. I can't remember the year, but I was so excited to attend ISPI's first Moving From Training to Performance workshop.

This incomplete list includes some of the evidenced-based, performance-oriented influencers whose work I enjoyed and learned from.

Biggest early influencers:

Bob Mager
Tom Gilbert
Geary Rummler
Alan Brache
Donald Kirkpatrick
Don Clark (Big Dog/Little Dog)
Joe Harless
Richard Swanson

Others in alphabetical order:

Roger Addison
Dale Brethower
Roger Chevalier
Dick Clark
Ruth Colvin Clark
Paul Elliott
Dana Gaines-Robinson
Roger Kaufman
Fred Nickols
Jack Phillips
Clark Quinn
James Robinson
Marc Rosenberg
Allison Rossett
Patti Shank
Howard Stolovitch
Will Thalheimer
Guy Wallace

What I learned about human performance technology and performance consulting made all the difference in my career. I focused on diagnostics, building effective solutions, implementing them in a way to improve performance, and measuring to prove I did (or learning when I needed to pivot and tweak things). In the sales profession, this turned out to be a key differentiator.

I remain puzzled and disappointed that performance consulting hasn't become as mainstream as I'd hoped it would. Leaders always seem to want to improve results. However, I'm often surprised by the lack of tolerance for the methods required to actually do so. It's a conundrum, for sure.

That said, I am encouraged by the sales enablement movement and how it's grown. The focus on sales enablement, especially as described in this book and as practiced in the more sophisticated sales organizations with mature sales enablement functions, has a tremendous amount of potential. Yes, the profession is evolving. Will we remain "sales enablement" or become revenue enablement, buyer enablement, commercial enablement, or performance enablement? My Magic 8-Ball says "Reply Hazy," but I do see an increased focus on improving sales outcomes versus just getting the basics in place. So, I'm hopeful that we will evolve sales enablement to sales performance consulting, whether by name or not.

What Is Performance Consulting?

Performance consulting is a systematic and holistic approach to improving workplace performance and achieving business goals. Performance consulting:

- Is grounded in analytics, diagnostics, and root cause analysis
- Considers of a broad array of organizational and individual factors that influence human performance
- Leads to the selection, design, and development of the most appropriate solution for an identified performance problem
- Implements solutions using proven-effective practices for the selected intervention and purposeful change management, including communication, follow through, measurement, analysis, evaluation, and adjustment to ensure you achieve the intended results

ATD offers a very robust human performance improvement model and various training programs, including the ATD Master Performance Consultant™ Program.

Whether you call it HPT, HPI, or performance consulting, the models all follow a general approach:

- A diagnostic phase with a gap analysis between the current state and desired future state
- A root-cause analysis to ensure you address the real cause of the performance gap
- A consideration for environmental, cultural, or other factors that influence performance
- A problem-solving design phase to ensure the solution addresses the root cause and the most effective solution is selected and designed
- Solution development
- Solution implementation with change management
- A way to measure progress to adjust as needed and evaluate results

This holistic performance orientation considers the best of what we've learned from other fields or practices, such as organization development, change management, Six Sigma, Lean Sigma, Total Quality Management, and industrial-organizational psychology.

This table shows some high-level differences between sales enablement and sales performance consulting.

	Sales Enablement	Sales Performance Consulting
Focus	Leading initiatives and projects	Addressing performance issues
Outputs	Activities include messaging, training, tools	Results include improved performance
Measures	Progress of initiatives and projects	Performance change and ROI
Assessments	How much the sales force uses outputs	How much the sales force improves
Accountability	Delivering things to the sales force	Delivering better sales productivity
Executive view	Cost center	Investment

Which side would *you* rather be on? It's definitely a journey from the left side to the right. Surprisingly, as I mentioned earlier, not all business leaders will care or want you to make the journey, mostly because they haven't seen anything like performance consulting in their past. For example, I've worked for executives who believed in training but didn't care if I did ROI evaluations. There are plenty who will care, though, and some who will truly get it, especially if you are able to produce business results. If we expect the sales enablement profession to continue to thrive, this is the path I believe we must take.

To be clear, I don't expect your sales enablement department to drive results on your own, or even with those you work with in cross-functional collaborations. Nor are you technically responsible for the performance of the sales force. You could do your very best work possible, and without the top-down support of your sales leader (and other executives), buy-in and coaching from front-line sales managers, and adoption by your sales force, the needle will not move. This is a team sport. However, you do have influence. Through that influence, performance consulting practices, and the building blocks and systems in this book, you can be part of the team (perhaps even the orchestra conductor) that has a massive impact on your company's performance. After all these years, that's the thing that still excites me most about the work we do.

If I could share one major lesson learned in my career about making this journey from enablement to performance consulting, it's this: Tailor your conversations with your executive team and senior sales leaders to the way they view the world. I've had managers with whom I could share the things from this chapter (and book), and they would be as excited as I am. With others, the eye rolls or snores would get in the way of my business case. With those leaders, focus on the outcomes they want, not the journey you'll have to take to get there. Of course, you'll need to get approval for a plan, but you can keep it at a high level.

The second piece of advice would be to carefully select where you work and seek places where you can do your best work and make an impact. Trust me; it's a lot more fun on the performance consulting side.

As you continue your journey with the sales enablement building blocks and systems thinking, keep this chapter in mind and create your personal learning plan to understand and incorporate the following into your work:

- Human performance technology
- Human performance improvement
- Performance consulting
- Organization development
- Organization behavior
- Organization effectiveness
- Lean and Six Sigma

- Agile methodology
- Change management

It's a road less traveled, but it will make all the difference.

Two roads diverged in a wood and I—I took the one less traveled by, and that has made all the difference. —ROBERT FROST

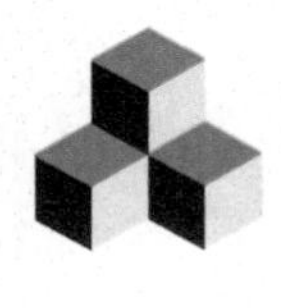

References and Recommended Resources

Systems Thinking

Cabrera, D., and L. Cabrera. 2018. *Systems Thinking Made Simple: New Hope for Solving Wicked Problems.* Plectica Publishing.

Rutherford, A. The Systems Thinker Series Book Series. amazon.com/gp/bookseries/B083BKYG7C/ref=dp_st_1083162101.

Buyer Acumen

Buyer Persona Development Masterclass. Training with Tony Zambito. tonyzambito.com/buyer-persona-development-master-class.

Revella, A. 2015. *Buyer Personas: How to Gain Insight Into your Customer's Expectations, Align your Marketing Strategies, and Win More Business.* New York: Wiley.

Buyer Engagement Content

Albee, A. 2015. *Digital Relevance: Developing Marketing Content and Strategies That Drive Results.* New York: Springer.

Sales Support Content

Rossett, A. 2006. *Job Aids and Performance Support: Moving From Knowledge in the Classroom to Knowledge Everywhere.* New York: Pfeiffer.

Sales Hiring

Kunkle, M. "Hire Sales Pros That Deliver Results." SPARXiQ e-book. sparxiq.com/ebook-hire-sales-pros-who-deliver-results.

SPARXiQ TalentGPS Sales Hiring Assessment. sparxiq.com/sales-talent-selection.

Wyatt, D. "5 Steps to More Effective Sales Hiring." SPARXiQ field guide. sparxiq.com/sales-hiring-5-effective-steps-field-guide.

Wyatt, D. "Look for These Traits in Your Next Salesperson." SPARXiQ field guide. sparxiq.com/sales-hiring-traits-field-guide.

Sales Training

Kunkle, M. "Sales Training That Sticks." SPARXiQ e-book. sparxiq.com/ebook-sales-training-that-sticks.

Kunkle, M., and J. Miller. "5 Stages to Ensure Your Training Sticks." SPARXiQ Infographic. go.sparxiq.com/ensure-sales-training-sticks-infographic.

Phillips, J., P.P. Phillips, and R. Robinson. 2013. *Measuring the Success of Sales Training*. Alexandria, VA: ATD Press.

Sales Coaching

Fournies, F.F. 2007. *Why Employees Don't Do What They're Supposed to Do and What to Do About It.* New York: McGraw-Hill Education.

Kunkle, M. "Sales Coaching Excellence." SPARXiQ e-book. sparxiq.com/sales-coaching-excellence.

Sales Process

Iannarino, A. 2017. *The Lost Art of Closing: Winning the Ten Commitments That Drive Sales.* New York: Portfolio/Penguin.

Jones, K., and S. Gielda. 2012. *Premeditated Selling: Tools for Developing the Right Strategy for Every Opportunity.* Alexandria, VA: ATD Press.

Kurlan, D. 2005. *Baseline Selling: How to Become a Sales Superstar by Using What You Already Know about the Game of Baseball.*

Thull, J. 2010. *Mastering the Complex Sale: How to Compete and Win When the Stakes are High!* New York: Wiley.

Sales Methodology

Kunkle, M., and D. Wyatt. 2020. "Shift to Buyer-Centric Selling." SPARXiQ cheat sheet, November 3. sparxiq.com/buyer-centric-selling-cheat-sheet.

Kunkle, M., and D. Wyatt. 2021. "Buyer-Centric Discovery." SPARXiQ cheat sheet, March 2. sparxiq.com/sales-discovery-cheat-sheet.

"Modern Sales Foundations." Sales methodology and training course. modernsalesfoundations.com.

Wyatt, D. 2021. "Effectively Communicate Four Types of Value to Your Buyers." SPARXiQ field guide, February 4. sparxiq.com/four-types-of-value-field-guide.

Sales Analytics and Metrics

Dearborn, J. 2015. *Data Driven: How Performance Analytics Delivers Extraordinary Sales Results.* Hoboken, NJ: John Wiley.

Dearborn, J. 2018. *The Data Driven Leader: A Powerful Approach to Delivering Measurable Business Impact Through People Analytics.* Hoboken, NJ: John Wiley.

Zoltners, A.A., P. Sinha, and S. Lorimer. 2015. *The Power of Sales Analytics.* Evanston, IL: ZS Associates.

Sales Technology and Tools

"Nancy Nardin Smart Selling Tools." Resource/service website. smartsellingtools.com.

"Vendor Neutral." Resources/service website. vendorneutral.com.

Sales Compensation

Cichelli, D. 2018. *Compensating the Sales Force, Third Edition: A Practical Guide to Designing Winning Sales Reward Programs.* New York: McGraw-Hill.

Donnolo, M. 2019. *Quotas! Design Thinking to Solve Your Biggest Sales Challenge.* Alexandria, VA.: ATD Press.

Zoltners, A., P. Sinha, and S. Lorimer. 2006. *The Complete Guide to Sales Force Incentive Compensation: How to Design and Implement Plans That Work.* New York: AMACOM.

Zoltners, A., P. Sinha, C. Albrecht, S. Marley, and S. Lorimer. 2017. *Sales Compensation Solutions: Addressing the Toughest Sales Incentive Issues in Today's Changing World.* Evanston, IL: ZS Associates.

Sales Manager Enablement

Brock, D.A. 2016. *Sales Manager Survival Guide: Lessons from Sales' Front Lines.* KCD Press.

Davis, K.F. 2017. *The Sales Manager's Guide to Greatness: 10 Essential Strategies for Leading Your Team to the Top.* Austin, TX: Greenleaf Book Group Press.

Hilbert, M.A., T. Travis, and J. Poulter. 2018. "Magic Quadrant for Sales Performance Management." Gartner, January 15. gartner.com/en/documents/3845264.

Travis, T., and M.A. Hilbert. 2018. "Critical Capabilities for Sales Performance Management." Gartner, January 17. gartner.com/en/documents/3846169.

Weinberg, M. 2015. *Sales Management. Simplified.* New York: AMACOM.

Zoltners, A.A., P. Sinha, and S. Lorimer. 2012. *Building a Winning Sales Management Team: The Force Behind the Sales Force.* Evanston, IL: ZS Associates.

Communication Management

"Information Mapping: Methodology." Website. informationmapping.com/pages/information-mapping-method.

Sales Support Services

"Books and E-Books by Naomi." Naomi Karten's website. nkarten.com/book2.html#HOW.

"Internal Service Level Agreement." Upcounsel website. upcounsel.com/internal-service-level-agreement.

Karten, N. 1994. *Managing Expectations.* New York: Dorset House Publishing.

Karten, N. 2002. *Communication Gaps and How to Close Them.* New York: Dorset House Publishing.

Karten, N. 2009. *Changing How You Manage and Communicate Change.* Cambridgeshire, UK: IT Governance Publishing.

Karten, N. 2010. *Presentation Skills for Technical Professionals.* Cambridgeshire, UK: IT Governance Publishing.

Getting Started and the Charter

"Getting Started in Sales Enablement." ATD digital booklet. learnmore.td.org/getting-started-in-sales-enablement-guidebook.

Sales Onboarding

Bray, C., and H. Sorey. 2019. *Hiring, Onboarding, and Ramping Salespeople: The T.E.A.M. Framework.*

Hale, J. 2011. *Performance-Based Certification: How to Design a Valid, Defensible, Cost-Effective Program.* Hoboken, NJ: Pfeiffer.

Kunkle, M. 2019. "Sales Onboarding With Mike." Slide presentation from ATD Sell 2019. sparxiq.com/event/sales-onboarding-atd-sell-2019.

Kunkle, M. 2021. "Why Your Sales Hires Aren't Ramping Up Sooner." SPARXiQ, January 21. sparxiq.com/why-sales-hires-arent-ramping-up-sooner.

HPT and Performance Consulting

ATD Master Performance Consultant Program. ATD certificate program. td.org/education-courses/atd-master-performance-consultant.

Pershing, J.A. 2006. *Handbook of Human Performance Technology.* New York: Pfeiffer.

Robinson, D.G., J.C. Robinson, J.J. Phillips, P.P. Phillips, and D. Handshaw. *Performance Consulting: A Strategic Process to Improve, Measure, and Sustain Organizational Results.* Oakland: Berrett-Koehler.

Rothwell, W.J. 2013. *Performance Consulting: Applying Performance Improvement in Human Resource Development.* New York: Wiley.

Rummler, G. 2007. *Serious Performance Consulting.* New York: Pfeiffer.

Rummler, G.A., and A.P. Brache. 2012. *Improving Performance: How to Manage the White Space on the Organization Chart.* San Francisco: Jossey-Bass.

Rummler, G.A., A.P. Brache, and R.A. Rummler. 2009. *White Space Revisited: Creating Value Through Process.* New York: Pfeiffer.

Stolovitch, H.D., and E.J. Keeps. 2004. *Training Ain't Performance.* Alexandria, VA: ATD Press.

Zoltners, A., P. Sinha, and G. Soltners. 2001. *The Complete Guide to Accelerating Sales Force Performance.* New York: AMACOM.

Other Sales Enablement Resources

Bray, C., and H. Sorey. 2017. *The Sales Enablement Playbook.*

"Certification Through Sales Enablement PRO." Sales Enablement PRO website. salesenablement.pro/certification.

Cohen, E. 2019. *Enablement Mastery.* Austin: Greenleaf Book Group Press.

Didner, P. 2018. *Effective Sales Enablement.* New York: Kogan Page.

Jefferson, R. 2021. *Sales Enablement 3.0: The Blueprint to Sales Enablement Excellence.* Roderick Jefferson and Associates.

Madian, T.M. 2020. *Enabler? I Hardly Know Her!: How to Make the Sales Experience Not Suck.*

Matthews, B., and T. Schenk. *Sales Enablement: A Master Framework to Engage, Equip, and Empower a World-Class Sales Force.* New York: Wiley.

"Sales Enablement Certificate." ATD certificate program. td.org/education-courses/sales-enablement-certificate.

Sisakhti, R. 2015. *Success in Selling.* Alexandria, VA: ATD Press.

Other Content From Mike

ATD blog posts and other content by Mike Kunkle, td.org/user/content/MikeKunkle.

LinkedIn articles by Mike Kunkle. bit.ly/MK-LinkedInArticles.

Sales Effectiveness Straight Talk webinar with Mike Kunkle. smmconnect.com/info/250.

SPARXiQ blog. sparxiq.com/tag/mike-kunkle.

Transforming Sales Results blog. mikekunkle.com/blog.

Index

About the Author

Mike Kunkle is a respected sales transformation architect and an internationally recognized expert on sales training, sales effectiveness, and sales enablement. He is the founder of Transforming Sales Results and is vice president of sales effectiveness services for SPARXiQ, where he advises clients, publishes thought leadership, speaks at conferences, leads webinars, designs sales training courses, delivers workshops, and designs and implements sales enablement systems that get results.

Mike has spent 36 years in the sales profession and 26 years as a corporate leader or consultant, helping companies drive dramatic revenue growth through best-in-class training strategies and proven-effective sales transformation methodologies and sales systems. At one company, as a result of six projects, he and his team enabled an accretive $398 million in revenue, year-over-year. At another, new sales reps with 120 days on the job were outperforming incumbent reps with five years with the company.

Mike collaborated with Doug Wyatt to develop SPARXiQ's Modern Sales Foundations curriculum and also authored SPARXiQ's Sales Coaching Excellence course. *The Building Blocks of Sales Enablement* is his first book.